DATE DUE

THE
RESURRECTION
OF ROME

﹏ THE ﹏
RESURRECTION
OF ROME

﹏   ﹏   ﹏

BY G. K. CHESTERTON

AUTHOR OF ﹏ THE EVERLASTING
MAN ﹏ THE THING ﹏ &C.

NEW YORK ﹏ DODD, MEAD
& COMPANY ﹏ MCMXXX

THE CONTENTS

I · THE OUTLINE OF A CITY

Before beginning this, the ten thousandth attempt at telling the most tremendous of all travellers' tales, it will be well to start with an apology. When it was first suggested to me that I should go to Rome and in some sense report upon the new transformations in that very old transformation-scene, I explained frankly that I am a very bad reporter; just as I am a very bad reviewer. And this is not in the least because I despise reporting or reviewing as dull; but because I find too much that is interesting in them and possess too little of the most interesting qualities they require: the qualities of selection and concentration. I am a bad reporter because everything seems to me worth reporting; and a bad reviewer because every sentence in every book suggests a separate essay. I can honestly say, as a general impression of things, that I never find anything dull, but a book describing the discovery that nothing is dull might be very dull indeed. In the same way I am bound, in telling my traveller's tale, to say that I am a bad traveller, or at least a bad tourist. And here again, I mean nothing but respect for the tourist; for the same is true of the pilgrim. I am naturally the sort of pilgrim who never sees the Pope because he stands too long staring at the Papal Guard. I speak here in a figure, for, as even these patchy pages will show, I did see the Pope; and my staring at the Papal Guard, which will be found described at intolerable length in a later chapter, did not occur till afterwards. But it is honestly quite true that I lack proportion, and my weakness as a traveller is that the world seems to me so amusing everywhere that it is hardly worth while to travel. When I start out for the ends of the earth, I am stopped on the road by an entertaining lamp-post or a wildly signalling window-blind; and have not even sufficient sense of the scale of difference between these passing questions and the Quest.

The same dramatic triviality troubles me when I actually reach a foreign land like Italy. If I honestly made a list of the things that do directly please my eye, it would seem crazy in exactly the fine old English sense of a crazy quilt or a crazy pavement. I do not know why it should please me that some of the broad black hats of the priests are all furry or hairy; but it does. I do not know why I should have the same sort of feeling for the squat palm-trees on which the porcupine fibres also look furry, as if they were animals instead of vegetables. Perhaps Miss Edith Sitwell would kindly explain why the tree is like the hat; I feel somehow that it would be in her line, though she would probably refer to the hairy sun and

the hairy moon in the course of explaining it. I do not
know why certain hard bluish cactus-leaves with teeth
make me feel (with great gratification) that I am walking at the bottom of the sea; or why I almost danced in
the street to see a tree growing on the top of a house; or
why, among rows of better and more famous busts, I like
the look of a Roman Emperor whose head is made of
black marble and his robe of red marble, as if he were a
negro with a tribal taste for gay and gorgeous garments.
If I were left to myself, these are the sort of things that I
should loiter about to look at; and such things may
turn up anywhere, even at home. But this, it is truly
said, is not seeing Rome. It is not, as will be remarked with increasing sternness, even writing about
Rome.

Well, I shall now pull myself together and write about
Rome. But, by way of completing the apology, I will
mention first the first thing I really noticed in Rome,
because it fixes exactly what I mean. I do not know
whether anybody else ever noticed it; I do not suppose
that most people would suppose it was worth noticing. I
have no idea how old it is, and I imagine it is quite new. I
do not know who did it or why, and I am not sure that
I even want to know; certainly I have not yet, as a fact,
taken the trouble to enquire. I am pretty sure it is in no
guide-book; and, what is more to the point, in no book
of more sensitive and individual impressions, like so
many that have been written about Rome. Yet the

[5]

thing was an event in my life—in that inner, infantile and fanciful life which begins with seeing the first Punch and Judy or owning the first air-gun. I merely walked across the road from my hotel, soon after my arrival, filled with no particular aspiration beyond a strong appetite for lunch; and just round the corner of the small street opposite I found a whole huge gateway carved like the face of a gigantic goblin with open jaws. It was rather like the Mouth of Hell in the mediæval pictures and plays. The worthy householder, who lived behind this pleasing façade, had presumably grown accustomed to popping in and out of the monster in the most prim and respectable manner. Whenever he went into his house he was devoured by a giant like the princesses in the fairy-tales. Whenever he came out of his house he was vomited forth by a hideous leviathan like the prophet in the story of Nineveh. This seemed to me rather quaint; I have never seen it anywhere else; I have never seen it mentioned here. Now of course I do know enough, in a smattering sort of way, to connect a thing of that sort with the antiquities or the novelties of Rome. Assuming my sternest air, as a guide to the tourist and the author of a serious book of travel, I can say that this is a remarkable example, and even extreme among the late extravagances of the Baroque. I shall in an instant plunge into a general survey in which there will be quite a lot of the Baroque. I merely wish to record that, while this little lane has a long name in Italian, which I

forget, I call it in my own mind Ogre Street; and my
adventures there are entirely my own.

Every town worth talking about has a shape; only the
great organized town-planned modern city has grown
shapeless. But then the great modern city is not worth
talking about; and nobody as a matter of fact ever does
talk about it, in the sense in which men will never leave
off talking about the town of Rye as much as the town
of Rome. Everybody knows that the precipitous terraces
of Edinburgh are like the profile of a particular human
face. Everybody who thinks of Bath thinks of the particular way in which particular grey crescents of houses
lie on particular green crescents of hills. There are aspects
in which Paris seems almost to stand in the Seine as
much as Venice in the sea; it is really the Island of the
City; and Notre Dame looks taller than the mere Eiffel
Tower. On the only occasion when I had ever been in
Rome, previous to the present visit, I found myself somehow in a position in which I missed this point—the
pointed outline of a particular and memorable place. I
was down on the lower level, where there is only a sensation of everything and everybody being canalized into
rather narrow streets, which are nevertheless supposed
to be the principal streets. There was a rather oppressive
feeling of everything being blocked up by the Victor
Emmanuel Monument, which, in comparison with
smaller and more interesting things, seemed to present
an Arctic wilderness of white marble, lit only with the

cold flame of gold. The traveller had a sense of running and dodging round the bewildering bulk of this monument and of not knowing what it was or where anything else was. Of course I saw the sights of Rome; but I never saw Rome, or discovered that Rome itself can be a sight. I could not find Rome anywhere; it seemed to have run away and hidden itself; probably behind one of the pillars of the Victor Emmanuel Monument. But on my second visit I found it quite suddenly and simply by the simple accident of having a room in an hotel on the great hill of the Trinità, which falls in a wide cascade of steps down to the level of the Corso. The position commands a splendid view of St. Peter's and the sunsets that clothe it every day; but it commands also something more special and perhaps more indescribable. There is a certain sensation of looking down into the chasms into which the seven hills are cloven; and a sense more or less irrational or imaginative that these chasms are very deep; and that something secret and subterranean is always rising like a sealed spring or a volcanic vapour out of the very depths of Rome. And this unreasonable image, like many unreasonable images, does represent a reality. It is the reality that was even realistically expressed when the investigators declared that they dared not excavate deeper under some of the Roman churches, lest the whole of Rome should cave in, and fall as if into an abyss. It is again what is very vividly suggested in the tradition, which is a true tradition, about the Lost Waters of the city; a mysterious buried river or shifting and vanishing fountain, which by its very name and nature hints once more at this haunting suggestion of profundity. Marion Crawford wrote a romance about that water and, by a very true artistic instinct, called it *The Heart of Rome*.

There is indeed something in that downward plunge of the mind that makes a man fancy that the heart might be so hidden; as if that evanescent fountain might be its fitful pulse or that dark river the very blood of the deep-hearted town. Looking down from the surrounding heights, we seem to see something written like a fiery hieroglyphic in the very lights of the city; something only to be conveyed in the old melodramatic tag: "Treasure is buried here." It is doubtless connected with the general fact of sunken antiquities and stratified foundations; and with more than one story of religions living like subterranean races. So the strange rites of the Persian sun-god were seldom practised in the sun; but always in caves, even if they were artificial caves; as when there flowed in the very foundations of St. Clement's that other dark river of the boiling blood of the Sacred Bull that was the purple sacrament of Mithras. So also another strange sect, sometimes confounded with that one, the men whose symbol was the Fish, lived a life that must have seemed like the blind life of fishes; except that in the eyes of their persecutors they were rather like poisonous rats living in the drains and sewers. It is that feeling, at least, which still gives its thrill of paradox to the story of the Catacombs. In the Catacombs at least there was truly a story of buried treasure.

Thus Rome looked to me like the City of the Seven Valleys. But to behold the mystery of the valleys it is necessary to stand on the hill. The whole effect, which I despair of describing, is somehow rather of depth than of height. It is the Gothic cities of the North that give the impression of height; the very lines of the architecture, as every one has noted, leading the eye upward to pointed roofs or tapering spires. It is not a question of actual but of relative height; though even in point of fact the spire of Old St. Paul's shot immeasurably far above the present classical building on Ludgate Hill. I am not ignorant of the fact that this impression could be contradicted in a material sense. My intelligence is equal to perceiving that the Colosseum is rather large; I know that St. Peter's is very high, and I have not commonly felt the need of the services of several kind Americans who have told me exactly how high. I know that, even in the more real world of imagination or impression, the place of the Gothic spires is to some extent taken by the straight converging lines of the great obelisks; and that a superb effect of height is sometimes reached by the great isolated columns, especially that one (to which I send all salutations and homage short of *latria*) on which the Mother of God rides triumphant upon the horns of the moon. But the general impression on my

memory remains what I say: the impression of not
ing up but down. Truth is not at the top of a tower,
really at the bottom of a well.

me is very notably, to the eye, a city of fountains.
not know whether there are really any more foun-
here than in other places; and once more I
teously wave away the assistance of the American
leman, eager to tell me that there are 321 more foun-
s in Tarentum, Neb., and 253 already planned for
kerton, Texas, when it shall have expanded to an
ropriate size. But the whole point of these things is
portion and prominence; and there is a strong effect
the streets of Rome of great fountains being at every
er corner; wreathed by the nymphs and ridden by
tritons of the most rampant moment of the Renais-
ce. And as I looked at them, there came vaguely
oss my mind the idea that these also were the perfect
pression of something, and that if the Lost Waters
re the heart, these fountains were the lungs of Rome.
d then I remembered that a fountain is itself a para-
x. It is a sort of topsy-turvy prodigy designed to show
at water can fall upwards or flow uphill. Water, which
as bowed and humbled, for all its brightness, amid the
cks where St. Francis could stroke it like a living thing,
here flung aloft like a flying thing; as if the well could
come a volcano. Water also was in a state of rebellion,
at least of resurrection. And when I found that word
ain, I knew the comparison that was haunting me;

I realized that Rome is Rome of the Fountains becau[se] there is in all of it this sense of secret things thrust upwards from below. The tritons might ride aloft as if they were gods of the sky rather than the sea; they might blow their shelly horns tossed up from the deep as if they were the trumpets of the dome; but their exultation was in having dragged up drowned things into the daylight and fished up sunken treasure to glitter in the strong sun of Italy.

That, I take it, is why the sevenfold city of hills does not strike us first as a city of heights. A dim imagination tells us that the buried pagoda of epochs is taller than any earthly tower. Or it is like some leviathan with protuberant eyes and nostrils standing out like mountains, but the rest of its immeasurable vastness veiled under the dark waters; a very prehistoric leviathan that did at last put out its nose to the hook of Peter the Fisherman. The City is unexhausted. The City is inexhaustible. But it is earthwards that it is an eternal city; and we find it by searching the chasm or looking downward to the dust. That, at least, is how it affected me and I do not instinctively think of this city as scaling the sky, half so much as many a narrow village church in Normandy or Northumbria. But I feel the sense of an inexhaustible store of superimposed cultures and closely packed secrets of the past; the sense of a place being mined for all the gold of human and divine glories; brought up for ever

out of an abyss of abundance, the depth and the rich-
ness of Rome.

That is the sort of summary that has come to stand in
my mind as corresponding to the outlines of the cities;
the steepness of Edinburgh or the great mirror of Venice.
And it is chiefly the effect produced, rightly or wrongly,
by standing on that hill called the Trinità di Monti and
looking across the valley to where the dome of St. Peter's
rises like a distant world. And indeed that impression is
perhaps increased now that it is in a new sense a distant
world in being in very truth a different nation. Beyond
the Tiber lies a land that is not Italy; at least that is not
merely Italy; and something mysterious in that new
creation, which corresponds to an old conception, in-
creases the sense of standing on the edge of a chasm and
looking out beyond the world. But anyhow, I never had
any such hint of the heart of the situation when I was
merely in the middle of the city. I owe it, not to myself
but to the high place on which I happened to stand, like
the goat in the fable; and if I were but one shade more
brazen and cynical a journalist than I am, I could have
written a whole book about Rome merely by looking out
of my window.

And as I looked down into these gorges or gullies of
the city sunken below me, glowing with lamps and alive
with crawling crowds and yet seeming in some dim way
like the lighted corridors of the Catacombs, there came
into my mind the shadow of a meaning which has fol-

lowed me in my wanderings ever since, and must serve
weakly as a sort of guide, not only for my wandering
feet, but for my much more wandering pen. It was the
general sense of something continually rising from below;
but especially of the continual rising of newer and newer
things, which are yet continually older and older. It
would be quite misleadingly depressing to talk of a
town of tombs. It would not perhaps be much more
cheery or cosy to talk of a town full of the special activi-
ties and agonies of premature burial. And yet there is
something of those two tragic elements in the effect; but
the effect is the very reverse of tragic. It is rather as if all
these valleys were open graves, and the graves were
open because the dead had never died. It seemed like a
place in which nothing was too old to be young. It was
as if the men of the Stone Age might stand up again like
the stone statues in the market; or the cave-men come out
painted and fantastic from their painted caves below. It
is a place where everything is buried and nothing is lost.
Therefore this mortuary imagery, that I have been
obliged to use, does not carry with it a mere savour of
mortality, but rather of immortality. I once amused
myself by some fancy or fairy-tale about a sort of goblin
war in the church-yard, between the tombstones carved
with a skull and the tombstones carved with a cherub
as representing the hopeless and the hopeful philosophies
of death. If Rome is a tomb or a place of tombs, it is
emphatically of the sort carved with a cherub; indeed we

can easily imagine it carved in the rather florid and tumid sort of Baroque that lends itself to the treatment of rather puffy cherubim. If I were to use the slang expression about a "dead alive" place, it would sound like the exact opposite of what I mean, and yet the words would mean literally exactly what I am trying to say. It is not a place where life is dull or dead or deadly; it is a place where the dead are alive.

I do not mean that it is a place where the mind can dreamily return to the past. I mean it is a place where the past can actually return to the present. I do not mean that it amuses me to imagine certain conditions that were there a few thousand years ago. I mean that I can quite well imagine some such conditions there a few thousand years hence. I mean that it has a sort of access to its own origins, and a power upon its own vanished youth, which is what is really meant by calling it The Eternal City. Those who used that term understood well enough that in one sense it is as vain as talking of the Immortal Suburb or the Everlasting Shop. They realized, much more vividly than do the moderns, that nothing earthly is eternal. But they expressed a real though relative truth; which is this unique capacity for renewal or the return of forgotten things. My own unfortunate religious prejudices would not indeed be gratified to see the Roman priests foretelling the future by examining the entrails of dogs and cats; or even watching whether the birds of the Campagna took the first to

[15]

the right or the second to the left. But I should not be the least surprised if the Italians did it, if once they had overcome those prejudices which they and I at present happen to share. Foretelling the future is a silly business anyhow, but it is quite as sensible to find it in the face of nature, or even the flight of birds, as in an arbitrary romance about a Utopia; and "a little bird told me" is as good an answer as any when we are asked for the authority of News from Nowhere. It would not please me personally to see anybody (with one or two doubtful exceptions) hurled from the Tarpeian Rock; but I should think it was quite possible that people might be again hurled from the Tarpeian Rock, if modern moral evolution and the emancipation of our ideals continues. In the same way, we may yet see an Imperator murdered in the Capitol or a Pope martyred in the Arena; but though they may be killed quite frequently, they will never be dead. In short, what I mean about Rome is that all of it was alive even when half of it was asleep. Which part of its past actually wakes up and walks about is more or less a question of circumstances; but almost any part of it could. And, just about the time of the Rome of which I write here, several parts of it did.

In a word; what I saw written across Rome was Resurgam; and I have taken that note or notion to be the nearest approximation to the theme of this book. As I looked across the ridges of the city, ranked like wave behind wave or wall within wall, there came more clearly into my mind the successive occasions in history on which this sunken wave has risen again like a wall. I remembered how Rome had fallen many times, and had been nearly destroyed by Hannibal before it destroyed Carthage, and was sacked by Alaric before its unarmed priest struck terror into Attila; how it had alternately won and lost in its wars with the Eastern and the Western Emperors; how it had defied extinction, how it had survived exile, how it had revived its ancient arts and was even now appealing to its ancient arms. And I fancied that, in attempting to explain some of the truth about modern Rome, I might take this general historical truth as a framework or an introduction; and arrange my explanation in a series of examples of such Roman revivals. I profess no special knowledge about Rome, and I shall not mention here even a hundredth part of the little that I do know. I am, as I have explained, a bad sightseer and possibly a blind traveller, and I shall not describe here even a hundredth part of the things that I did see. But I do still think that it is a question of something to be explained; and that there are many who have seen much more and understand much less. I do not think it is easy for Englishmen or northerners in general to understand Rome. I do not think it is at all easy for them to like Rome. I think there is a real, primary and perfectly honest difficulty staring them in the face at the start; and, after some little thought and doubt, I decided to attack it at the start.

The shortest way of putting the problem is that the Rome we see is truly and even obtrusively a Papal town. You may add fire to the phrase, if you will, by calling it a Papist town; but I do not in the least mean merely a Roman Catholic town. Multitudes of sympathetic and enlightened northerners can recognize that Oberammergau or Assisi is a Roman Catholic town, without in the least losing their sympathy for it. But Rome is Papal; it strikes the eye first of all as a town built of triumphal arches to welcome Popes or towering tombs to commemorate Popes: and those chiefly the Popes who have the worst name outside their own communion; the Popes of the Renaissance. Of course any Protestants can, and some Protestants do, proudly demonstrate their Protestantism by looking only at the remains of Paganism. Any Englishmen who choose may rush through Rome, looking neither to the left nor to the right, till they have hidden their heads in the Well of Vesta or washed themselves clean of all Christian contacts in the Baths of Caracalla. Similarly any Italians can, if they like, fly northward in a completely closed aeroplane and take no notice of England until they can alight for half an hour's inspection of Stonehenge. If they were careful to avert their eyes so as not even to catch a glimpse of the spire of Salisbury Cathedral, they would be behaving very much as some Anglo-Saxons have behaved towards the superstitions of the Holy City they have come hundreds of miles to see. But the students of Stonehenge could hardly be said to have seen England, let alone London; and the students of Roman antiquities have not really been in Rome. I do not imagine, however, that there are many of these purely Paganizing Protestants among my readers, or indeed anywhere else; and for sensible and reasonably friendly Protestants the real problem does remain. How are they *really* to like something that looks like an enormous marble monument to glorify what they don't like? It is not only that Rome is Papal, but that it is so obviously proud of being Papal. True, this is not because the Pope is proud, but because of the mysterious circumstance that a large number of people are proud of the Pope. But why are they proud of the Pope? How could anybody be proud of a Pope? Such murmurs, now largely subconscious, seemed yet audible. And, after brooding darkly for days, I decided to attempt to answer the first question first. I would attempt it by way of historical example.

I resolved to begin frankly with St. Peter's; the eternal rock of offence; to the Puritans a stumbling-block and to the æsthetes foolishness. I gravely doubt if my brethren really like all those shiny marbles and showy statues; but I might begin to explain why the Romans liked them. And then it occurred to me that the decision of an ancient Pope was really responsible for the existence of these statues; perhaps of any statues. It seemed an excellent text for explaining the part that Papal Rome played in history; I therefore concluded the first chapter by telling the forgotten story of the Pope and the Iconoclasts.

Then there burst on me, I confess, the huge and impossible task I had taken on. I had begun naturally with one example; because he who broke the Iconoclasts sowed the seed of the Renaissance. But, by that example, I seemed committed to write a whole history of Christendom, with all the Church's decisions, in order to explain a few fluted columns or coiling cornucopias. Then it struck me that St. John Lateran, which naturally comes second to St. Peter's, does by a curious accident telescope the mediæval and the modern. It contains the tomb of a Pope who pronounced on the greatest popular movement of the thirteenth century; and also of one who pronounced on the popular movements of to-day. I therefore used this chapter as a sort of bridge or summary. But indeed the modern and the mediæval lie very close. The modern world is largely divided into two sorts of mediævalists; the silly æsthetes who think it very modern to be mediæval and the good craftsmen who have realized that it is very mediæval to be modern.

This, I thought, will bring us to the Renaissance; the popular and obvious example of the Resurrection. And it will bring us back to the direct consideration of the outstanding monuments of Rome. The interlude of mediævalism had to be abstract; for Rome has hardly anything mediæval in the concrete. But the Renaissance is more concrete than some refined persons can endure without being seriously unwell. There is no point in connecting one Roman church with the Renaissance; for practically all the Roman churches are Renaissance churches. But I attempt to reconcile my brethren of the north, the readers of Ruskin, the fleers from Rubens, to something more heroic and not altogether so heathen in the whole conception of the Renaissance itself. It was, after all, one of the supreme examples of Roman civilization possessing this power of resurrection; and resurrection is not material, but mystical; not a result of doubt but rather of faith; not a mere contempt of the past, but rather an invocation; a sort of wild veneration for the dead.

From this we pass to the Baroque, the last and most theatrical phase of the Renaissance; and here again I note that it is parallel to another historical phase of the Church. There was a reason in the theology of the seventeenth century for cherubs being allowed to kick and saints to caper quite so much as all that; just as there was a reason in the theology of the Dark Ages for their being allowed to appear at all. In short, it is my general aim throughout to show that all these artistic manifestations spring from deep spiritual energies in the religious centre itself; and that is why they seem, at first sight, to be almost insolently proud of that centre as a centre of civilization. As types and tastes stand to-day, we must begin with the reason for the exuberant, or it will seem to us merely exuberance. Many men must understand why

Rome was wonderful before they can see that it is beautiful.

Finally, I have devoted the last two sections to the last two modern manifestations of this principle of old things reappearing as new things. They have both occurred quite recently; and one very recently. The first, which I have called *The Return of the Romans* is concerned with Fascism; and especially with that aspect of Fascism that is really symbolized by the Fasces. I mean the impulse to recall what up to that moment seemed most remote from all modern thought; the old Roman ideas of dignity and authority and the re-erection of the far-off imperial ensigns and salutes. Here again, without at all approving of everything in the reaction, I have tried to explain to those who disapprove, why, as I think, it did so sharply and violently react. Anyhow, whatever else it is, it is an exact example of what I mean; the sudden appearance of something so old as to be almost forgotten and so new as to be entirely unexpected. And I have given the last chapter to the last example; the reappearance in Europe of a Papal State, of the Pope as a secular prince in the council of kings; a typical example of something which forty years ago men would have been certain could return no more. Having begun with the attempt to explain to the fair-minded outsider something of the intelligible case for a Papal town, I shall at the end dwell somewhat more fully on the ideas that justify a Papal State. This book, which I fear will seem

[22]

very sprawling and shapeless in any case, will be quite
unintelligible unless it is understood that I am throughout addressing that sort of fair-minded outsider, only
hoping to persuade him that the thing is great even from
the outside; by telling him some things he may not have
realized about the greatness to be found in the inside.
I am not asking him to come inside. Whatever he may
think, I am not now trying to make him a convert; I
am only trying to make him a happy and successful tourist. But I have come to the conclusion that no tourist
will be happy and successful in Rome if he is merely
shown gilded wreaths and twisted trumpets. They will
generally repel him unless he understands what sort of
triumph of truth, truly or falsely, the Popes imagined
they were adorning when they modelled it so boldly
upon the triumphs of the Cæsars. Nobody can understand
the triumphs and the trophies when he has never heard
of the battles; and the battles were nearly all intellectual
and won by the Sword of the Spirit. That is why I have
begun this book with the Emperor who denounced the
Idols and ended it with the Dictator who enthroned the
Pope.

That is the general direction in which my mind has
here moved, or perhaps wandered; and yet I feel that it
misses the point. It is rather what I shall have written
than what I intend to write. For something much larger
and more luminous was with me as I looked under that
large and luminous evening sky across the main valley

of Rome; and my sense was not of a series but rather of one thing terribly instantaneous. Even with that word Resurrection, it seemed as if the very landscape altered; in a manner beyond all the normal changes of day and night. The pale and quiet daylight of that day took on for a moment the light of something catastrophic, and I saw a high place of the world that something had stricken immortal, and yet for ever in the throes of gestation and the pride of procreative death. It seemed as if that moment would never end; as if the chasms were like cracks in a world rigid with the crack of doom; with the rending of the mountains and the rising of the dead.

To put it better, and more briefly, I suddenly saw lie open before me a book that I cannot write. This book is the printed proof that I cannot write it. I could, I suppose, if I liked, go back and write another book, full of the details of Rome and the hundred accidents of travel; I might describe, not quite so well as others have done it, the great road that goes forth from Rome lined with the long series of ancient Roman ruins as with the deployment of a crippled Roman army. I might recall the mighty circle of distances to be seen from the height of Rocca di Papa, where it hangs like a city built for eagles; or the Hill of Tusculum or the skeleton of Ostia against the sea. I might labour through the thousand exhausting excitements with which the city itself is honeycombed; or go mad counting the churches in Rome. Or I might

begin again and write a better book about all the human
contacts of the place, and the curious and interesting persons to be found there. I might tell the story of the intensely interesting Frenchman, who began by being a
Huguenot horribly shocked at the High Churchmen in
England, and ultimately went over to Rome by the unusual route of an admiration for Mr. Gladstone. Or I
might describe the delightful Irish abbot, hidden in an
almost subterranean Italian church, with whom I discussed all my Dublin friends in a dark crypt before an
altar of Mithras; and in whom I proved again the mysterious truth that every Irishman is silently laughing at
every other Irishman; I never can imagine why, when
they have the English to laugh at. Or I might speak of
the English lady who assumed that I believed in Reincarnation because I was an Englishman; or the lady
journalist, also an ornament of my country, who had
never heard that Parliamentary politics are corrupt. A
greater obligation, and an even greater pleasure, would lie
in acknowledging all the forms of hospitality and courtesy which I received, if they were not too numerous to
be acknowledged; to offer my thanks to those of my
countrymen who introduced me to so delightful an English circle in Rome; and especially to the diplomatist
whose children made such resounding speeches to the
Bambino; to the generous American student who would
have assisted me to enter, I might almost say to burgle,
the church of Santa Maria sopra Minerva, and whom I

afterwards ill-repaid by making a speech at him, and all his brethren of the American College, people who certainly contradicted the slander that a man cannot be a real Catholic and a real American; to the repeated hospitalities of the English College and the Beda; to the Rector of the Scotch College, whose good officers are acknowledged elsewhere, and all his critical but genial congregation; and to the delightful Irish Franciscans who almost persuaded me that St. Francis must have been an Irishman. Perhaps the most impressive incident, which would require a book to itself, was the experience of visiting the College of Propaganda, with its friendly crowd of every race and colour under heaven; a real League of Nations—which did not quarrel. On some, and possibly many, of these incidents or aspects I shall touch in their turn; but I am conscious that I could have written a much more amusing book if I had confined myself entirely to these many-coloured experiences. And yet something moves me to attempt to complete somehow, or rather to deal with incompletely, the general historical or philosophical notion I had in mind, as I looked on that luminous evening from the obelisk of the Trinità across to the dome of St. Peter's. Only the complete thing I had seen broke as I saw it; and all that follows here is but a litter of the fragments.

"When falls the Colosseum Rome shall fall." All have read the statement in elegant extracts; a few in Byron; fewer still in St. Augustine, who, I am told, first records the proverb. I do not believe it: not even to please St. Augustine, let alone Byron. The Colosseum could fall without killing Rome, or even the Romans, though not (it is pleasant to think) without killing a large number of American and other foreign tourists, mostly rich. I should escape callously, for I do not haunt the Colosseum, least of all by moonlight. I am not and never was a ghost. As already noted there is almost a contradiction between seeing Rome and seeing the sights of Rome. There are bold and brilliant adventurers who can do both; but the one does not necessitate and hardly helps the other. The Roman sights could be taken from Rome and put inside Ramsgate, and they would still be sights, but they would not be Roman. The Colosseum might be rebuilt on the site of Olympia, an appropriately classic name for a competitive arena. The Baths of Diocletian might be moved to Bath or Baden, or other places where the Roman Bath would be really appropriate enough. But it is not only obvious that West Kensington would not look like Rome; it is even more obvious that, without these or thirty other famous buildings, Rome would still look like Rome. This common quality that really colours a town, and makes it a contrast to other towns, is never easy to define. But broadly speaking, what bulks big in the eye of a visitor to the Italian capital is all that incidental magnificence, of pillars and public fountains and round Roman gateways, which seems sprinkled everywhere between the recognized sights of the sightseer. These secondary splendours are nearly all of one period and in one style. They are in that florid form of the classic which filled Europe, with increasing luxuriance though often with lessening merit, from the beginning of the sixteenth to the end of the eighteenth century. These are the things that stamp Rome as the Gothic stamps Rouen or Nuremberg; a man who likes this sort of thing will probably like Rome; a man who heartily dislikes it will heartily dislike Rome; and I shall not think the worse of him for saying so.

On nearly all these civic monuments or trophies, the stranger will soon see in old but large and lucid lettering, very widely spaced and very majestically designed, at least some fragment like the phrase "Pontifex Max." and the more sensitive Puritan will once more find himself in the presence of the subtle machinations of the Pope. The Papal conspiracy is not perhaps quite so covert or underground as he has been given to understand. In these very large letters there is some failure in Jesuitical discretion; and, before the end of his visit, he will probably find himself abusing the Popes for exactly the opposite reason to his old one; a change of attack to which Popes have grown somewhat accustomed from of old. He will feel most probably, and not unnaturally or unreasonably, that there is something quite appallingly pagan and presumptuous about this brazen blazoning everywhere of the title of a Vicar of Christ. I can quite understand that feeling, and I am not making fun of it. There is an answer; but there is a question, and it is on the face of it a fair question. A great part of this book will necessarily be devoted to answering it. But at this stage I am not merely impatient with the Puritan for being shocked. Rather do I desire to lead him by the hand into inner circles of the city, where he will be more shocked. I wish him indeed to begin at the other end and the very extreme of what he finds shocking in the central temple of Papal Rome where the dreadful pontiffs seem to be demonstrative even in death. We talk of things silent as the grave; we can hardly say of these graves that they are even silent. And I put the paradox here because I wish the critic to consider first a certain special type of art and especially of sculpture. Many have said that architecture is frozen music. I would suggest a sort of statuary that is like frozen rhetoric.

I will leave the True Christian to labour a very obvious

contrast between St. Peter's and St. Peter. As a matter of
fact, like many laboured and obvious things, it is not
so true as it looks. Simon Peter was probably a simple
man; but men often dislike pomp or splendour because
they are not simple enough to like it. No notes were made
at the time about the great Fisherman's taste in architecture, his friends being otherwise employed on matters
which they (being also simple men) fancied to be more
urgent. But if he had any particular admiration for any
particular building, I should say he is as likely as not
to have been thrilled, in a deplorably theatrical manner,
by the florid Corinthian magnificence of the Herodian
Temple. And if to-morrow morning a Neapolitan fisherman, fresh from the nets and in exactly the same child-
like spirit as Simon of Galilee, made his first journey
from the sea to Rome, I strongly suspect that he would
throw up his hands in wonder as Michael Angelo intended him to do. For all art is sensational, since it aims
at producing some sort of sensation. There are other
examples of the fact that the simple may see subtle things,
even after the subtle have so long lectured and laid down
the law about rather simple things. It is a simple and
self-evident thing, for instance, that the great shrine of
the Fisherman is "inlaid with gorgeous marbles" or "en-
crusted with gold and many-coloured stones." It is perhaps less simple, but even more true, that in spite of this
luxurious licence and variegation, a common tone is
somehow kept, which is at once predominant and yet

quiet. A scheme of colour in itself temperate and simple, a sort of pearly grey picked out with a singular sort of dark chocolate red, does manage to master and unify the whole building and make the gaudiest of the incidental colours merely incidental. Secondly, the same severe northern critic will certainly criticize the Tombs of the Popes, with all the more severity because he does not know which is which, and has probably never heard of any of them before. He sees the Holy Fathers are all gesticulating in a turbulent Italian fashion, and enjoys all the advantages of not having a notion of what they are gesticulating about. But even he would think it odd if Richard the First, waving a sword at Westminster, were jeered at by a savage who had never even heard of the Crusades; or foreigners pointed at the baton of Wellington without even knowing that it might be pointed at Waterloo. And if the critic will condescend to examine the admirably carved reliefs in the entablatures before the tombs (all of them fine pieces in craftsmanship of their own kind) there will gradually dawn, upon his dizzy and reeling senses, the suggestion that the Popes of Rome have really had to do with rather important incidents in the history of the world. He will find one presiding over the terrestrial globes and the great geographical explorations that made the modern world; another establishing buildings and galleries that are still the glory of the world; and one of the last, and most pathetic, praying to Our Lady to lift up the Holy Child

[33]

over a grim and graven background of the whole dim pandemonium of the Great War. We may agree or disagree with these posturing pontiffs, but they were not provincial or even private; they had rather a way of being in the middle of things. Lastly, there is a quality about this posturing, if you call it posturing, which it is quite vital to understand if we are to understand anything about Italy or the Italian spirit. In some aspects it is called vivacity. In this aspect, and for my purpose, it is perhaps most true to call it oratory. These Popes are orators in stone, and all this sculpture is rhetorical sculpture. And those who dislike it, or dismiss it, go off and gaze with owlish reverence at the old pagan Forum; and buy large brown photographs of the Forum, which make it look much larger than it is, to hang in their drawing-rooms. And it never once occurs to them to remember that the old Romans were Italians; or to ask what a Forum was for.

As I shall mention more than once, I know all that there is to be said against the rococo quality of the Renaissance. It did marvels in statuary, or sculpture in the round; but many may feel that the statues are rather too round. It blinded the world with a blaze of white marble that was like so much frozen and solidified light. But many wish it were no more solidified than snow and that all the marble gods might melt with the Snow Man of Michael Angelo. I am not now debating or defending these things; I am trying to disentangle a certain element which is not debated or defended or even often detected, but which is of the soil and is dug up like the marble in the mountains of Italy. We all remember the carelessness which Macaulay carelessly attributed to the ancient Romans:

> The stone that breathes and struggles,
> The brass that seems to speak—
> Such cunning they who dwell on high
> Have given unto the Greek.

It would be truer to say that they have given it to the Roman. It is a much more correct description of the art to be found in Rome. The Venus of Milo does not struggle; and it is the very power of her presence that she hardly seems to breathe. There are of course in all these things complexities that confuse generalizations. But the Greeks began, as we know, by proclaiming that there must be severe statues, and ended, as we shall see, by saying that there must be no statues. There ran through all Hellas, even in its most humanistic moment, a certain stern simplification, and a calm like waking sleep, which may have been affected by lying so close under the shadow of the erect and rigid gods of Egypt and the East. Anyhow "the stone that breathes and struggles" does not describe even the Elgin Marbles, which are full of trampling horsemen and wrestling centaurs. But it does describe the Papal Tombs in St. Peter's at Rome, though they deal with holy and hoary men dead and at rest in the Lord, but exhibit them alive with thunderous brows and hands uplifted as if with thunderbolts; as positive as despots; as passionate as demagogues. The stone breathes and struggles and breaks out into great cries almost audible down the ages; for these are the statues of the sacred orators of Italy; the speakers of the Word that is given *urbi et orbi;* the men who spoke as princes to the city and as priests to the world. "If these were silent the very stones would cry out."

I know it is not easy for my countrymen to seize this aspect. On the general subject of Popes, there are a good many things they do not know, and a good many things they optimistically think they know. They have heard of Alexander Borgia; and deduced that all Cardinals have been commonly occupied in poisoning each other. They have never heard of Francis Borgia; or of countless Popes who were quite as humble and simple as Francis Borgia. They do not know that many, even of these Papal patrons of the Baroque, who heaped on their dead predecessors mountains of marble and gold, or interlaced the labyrinth of the city with traceries of the Dionysian vine or the Apollonian laurel, were themselves men of pure manners and of abstemious diet, living like hermits in comparison with many a British merchant, or even Baptist minister, whose London was a nightmare of chimneys and chimney-pot hats, but whose own mahogany groaned under all the luxuries that greed or gluttony could demand. The Popes fasted and made their city beautiful;

[36]

the Puritans feasted and left their city hideous. This may
be one-sided, but it is the side we turn to the wall. The
rococo temple may be vulgar; but even this tawdry trifle
of Michael Angelo is not much uglier than the brick
Bethels and Emmanuels of Manchester built after two
hundred years of further intellectual progress. And if,
alas, civilization means luxury, it sometimes means taste;
and not all advantages are with the taste of tea and muf-
fins. Anyhow, the Pontiffs were great patrons of sculpture. Each one who stands here a statue ordered the
statue of another, leaving a stone pedigree like a procession of statues. One of them was responsible for rais-
ing, or trying to raise, that incredible army of statues,
which was to occupy the city like a multitudinous invasion of the gods; and of which one or two remain,
not altogether unnoticed, like monsters after a flood; such
as that strange horned and bearded god or monster to
whom his great maker gave the name of Moses. And yet
I am not thinking of the statue-makers or the patrons
of statuary, but of one who long before, in dim and distant centuries, stood at the beginning of the story of the
statues.

My mind goes back, amid all these marble monuments,
to another Pontifex Maximus, who I suppose has no such
monument; certainly no such prominent monument; and
who lived in days when no such monuments could exist
even in a dream. And yet he stands in history as the
founder of this great city of the statues, and, after that

monumental fashion, the maker of Rome. But for him, and those who maintained his policy, this town that teems around me with lively imagery, good, bad and indifferent, would now be as naked as a Pyramid and as featureless as a Quaker burial-ground. And because this story of the stand he made, and its creative consequences, is very little known even in educated England, I propose to pause upon it here. I should like to do a little popular justice to the dim and dusty figures of those stiff archaic pontiffs who, when all our own world was as yet practically undiscovered, determined the course of history and saved us before we were born. For all this sculpture, which is here called oratorical, is in very truth the reverberations of a voice. All this struggling stone, all these marble masks "that seem to speak," do indeed depend through all ages on a spoken word; and the priests who look down on us like judges are here through a single judgment long ago.

If we could undo the past . . . if that word could be unsaid—then indeed all this too, too solid marble would melt and flow back to the mountains, and the columns wilt like withered stalks, and the City of the Fountains dry up and disappear. That image of an imageless town, and Tiber unvisited, must be my excuse for selecting here one example out of many; the debate on Images which shaped Christendom and therefore the modern world. It may seem odd that the story of our culture should begin with the Image-Breakers and end with the

Imagists. But it is not for nothing, even in literature, that we Europeans talk always of imagery and of figures of speech. It is not for nothing that even those who blame Image-Worship will praise Imagination. Anyhow, here is the story, and it proves one thing at least. When the world was fanatical, the Church was moderate. Or (if you prefer it so) when the Church was fanatical, the Pope was moderate.

Mr. H. G. Wells had the misfortune to write an Outline of History having in his heart two hearty detestations; a hatred of Pagan Rome and a hatred of Christian Rome. Were I to step out of my common course and write an Outline of Science, being consumed with a contempt for the subjects of Matter and Force, or an Outline of Darwinian Evolution, having an exquisitely balanced loathing for monkeys and men, or an Outline of Chemistry when I could not contain myself for fury at the very thought of oxygen or hydrogen or any of the chemical elements, my misfortunes in these various fields would certainly be far worse than his. He is in that sense to be congratulated on having come through so triumphantly, and written a most interesting book in spite of his disgust with nearly all the most interesting things in it. The double disgust in this case is somewhat unusual. Some rather narrow Catholics have exaggerated the horrors of heathen Rome, but even the narrowest had a broad field of human sympathy among the very varied saints and doctors of Christian Rome. Some even more narrow sceptics, of the type of Gibbon or Middleton, have similarly exaggerated the Christian faults; but these were generally the very men who delighted in stately salutations to the stoical heathen virtues. To make a quintessence of narrowness, out of the intersection of these two narrow views, has been reserved for that modern man of genius who is never tired of telling us to cultivate a wider outlook and stretch out "to something larger than all this." He has rather the appearance of being pushed towards this blank future by a process of elimination, though it seems possible that it is the future that will be eliminated. A traditionalist will be tempted to ask of many Futurists, "If a man does not love men whom he has seen, how shall he love Supermen whom he has not seen?" These matters, however, are not in question here; and I will only claim to write of Rome in so far as I think I can understand heathens better than he can Catholics. But his name and example occurred to me in connection with the idea of an Outline of History; because I had a sense of penitence or relenting towards him and a disposition to unsay much I had said when I found how frightfully difficult even a small section of an Outline is to draw. I feel it specially difficult in relation to the historical incidents in the quarrel of Rome and Byzantium, on which depended, I think, not only our own destiny but even our own existence.

Very broadly, however, the determining events were these. The Empress Helena, like several Roman ladies, was a Catholic by private conversion and undoubtedly by the most personal conviction and devotion. She persuaded her son Constantine the Great to become a Catholic; but, although the whole matter is disputed, it is not unfair to say that it was probably less of a personal and more of a political conversion. By which I do not mean a vulgar sneer, in the style of the modern imitators of Gibbon, to the effect that he was a humbug with an axe to grind. I mean rather what many such moderns would regard as a compliment; that he was thinking rather more of saving his empire than of saving his soul. He was a soldier and a statesman and not a humbug; and if he had an axe to grind, it was at least the ancient axe of the Fasces of Rome. And yet it came about that he deserted Rome because he was so very Roman.

The riddle is read thus. Two needs or tendencies were apparent to him; on which his curious double action was taken. The first was the feeling which the wiser Stoic Emperors must have had; that the queer patchwork world, which was now one realm, really needed one religion; probably combined with the feeling of how perfectly hopeless for that purpose was the religion of the Stoic Emperors and the Stoics. Marcus Aurelius rides the high horse with his high ideals on the high place of the Capitol. But when I saw his head against blue sky I knew I had seen that profile in many Ethical Societies. I respect it and him, but you cannot get a corporate confession and communion out of that woolly-headed,

woolly-bearded, woolly-witted moralist. The religion must
be a religion, and not a philosophy; at the same time it
could not merely be a cult, for the cults were all local and
many of them lawless. To quote Mr. Wells again, if Men
are like Gods, we would like to know which Gods; and
whether Man is to be Moloch the murderer or Mercury
the thief. And the second element which affected him
and all his time was what may be called, in a modern
political phrase, the Drag Towards the East. As the
Roman Empire solidified into one civilization, it became
apparent that the East was the more civilized end of it.
The rich ruins of Egypt and Babylon counted more
than the German forests or the remote British islands.
But there was something much deeper than that in the
oriental trend. Men did not then use such words of it;
but the East was powerful because the mind of man
was once more becoming mystical. It was not in itself necessarily an improvement. The best men and the
worst men are mystics; and the innocent materialist is
better than the last, as worse than the first. And the Mystery out of the East might have had too much of the wisdom of the Serpent rather than the purity of the Dove.
But what the Augurs saw was the Dove turning back the
Eagles.

Anyhow, Constantine under this oriental influence did
two very strange and symbolic things; things that have
changed the world and will be remembered to the last
records of men; but perhaps remembered rather than

understood. First, of course, he proclaimed the New Religion in Rome. He accepted, or half accepted, like a man dazzled by new light, the vision that advanced towards him out of the East, which had stricken Saul prostrate upon the road to Damascus and sundered Augustine from the ancient schools of Athens. This was in itself a thing to stagger the stars, for all those who knew how deep in that deep rock was the old civic religion of Rome, and how every detail of life in antiquity was interlaced with rituals and guarded by gods. A Roman might more readily have understood an edict establishing a new sun and moon, or proclaiming that henceforward winter must come immediately after spring, as imagine that his piety and his pride were no longer to revolve round the Temple of Vesta or the thunderous god of the Capitoline Rock. The thing is done for ever, and no man born will ever now realize how strange it was. But the other thing that Constantine did has always seemed to me even stranger. And it is part of something not only mystical but enigmatic in the whole matter that these two acts were done by one man in one reign; and it is possible that as the one was the beginning of all Christian triumphs, so the other was the beginning of all Christian tragedies.

He did not only welcome this Eastern mystery as it moved westward towards the rock of Rome. He conceived the extraordinary idea of moving Rome eastward, as if to meet it halfway. He conceived the idea of tear-

ing up the rock and moving it like a rolling stone towards the sunrise and the strange deserts where the New
God had been born. It was almost as if the oriental influence had blown upon Rome of the stubborn stones
and landmarks, the fenced fields and the sacred walls,
something of that nomadic and wandering spirit that
belonged to the desert peoples. He seems to have fancied
that he could shift the palace like a pavilion and lead
forth the immemorial Capitol like a caravan. Romans
had known the city built of brick and the city built of
marble, and now they were almost commanded to fold
their tents like the Arabs. There must have been some
unearthly atmosphere of unrest everywhere that made
the notion seem possible. As the Three Kings came out
of the East bearing gifts of gold and incense, the greatest
King of all the kings of the earth might have been represented in some painted parable as coming out of the
West bearing gifts of marble and mighty bronze; holding in one hand the Arch of Titus and in the other the
Temple of Vesta. For though he did not move such
things materially, this is in truth what he did morally;
he uprooted and transplanted Rome. He took away all
that made the sacred city sacred in its pagan past; the
great palace and the Senate and the Legions and the
golden eagles of Cæsar. And he set these things up again
in a strange land towards the skies of morning, upon the
Golden Horn in the far country of the Greeks. He left

with a New Religion. He may well have seen the rise of the New Rome out of the earth almost as hopefully as St. John saw the descent of the New Jerusalem out of the skies. But there was a difference. St. John interposed between himself and his perfect township an incidental detail or condition called the end of the world. It is the custom of the small-headed prigs who explain away the Christian origins to scoff in an amusingly lofty manner at the poor Early Christians, because in their superstition they imagined that the end of the world was coming. The Early Christians were much nearer the truth than Constantine.

Old Rome was left behind almost like a ruin; it is a symbol but hardly an exaggerative one to say that grass grew in the streets and even in the temples. The decline was long masked by the balancing of Eastern by Western Emperors; but the Eastern eventually extinguished or annexed the Western. Those acquainted with popular history who talk of the two great periods of Rome's material and moral empire, the Rome of the Cæsars and the Rome of the Popes, are often oblivious or unconscious of this curious interlude of the widowhood and desertion of Rome, of the weedy neglect and provincial stagnation. As men say that the jungle makes a silent invasion of a dead city, so the vast vague savagery of Western Europe, still in a great degree nameless and nationless and nomadic, drifted through and wasted and discoloured this dead city of the Tiber and the Tarpeian Rock. Perhaps, by way of another symbol, we may say that Rome above ground might have rotted, but Rome underground remained; the Catacombs or the prison of the martyrs. But the broad historical fact, on which turned such immense destinies of history, can be stated simply enough. The Emperor of Rome had left Rome; but the Bishop of Rome had not.

Anybody can see, in this strange situation, what silent question was really put to the world. Cæsar, moving eastward, had taken the whole world with him. If anything was left, like a ghost in an empty house, it was something not of the world. The purely practical claim of Rome against Byzantium was so futile on the face of it that it is hard to find a parallel. But suppose that, tomorrow morning, the Dean of Winchester were to announce that his town was of larger importance than London, and was the one great political centre of the whole British Empire, he would be rather in the position of the Pope pleading for the Old Rome against the New Rome. Winchester once really was the capital of England; but most Englishmen have forgotten the fact for some little time. The actual present resources of Winchester, for sustaining the part of London, are not large. But English towns are all close together and in a compact mass of civilization. Rome and Byzantium were divided by seas and deserts and bounded to the west by a world still wild and unknown, only partially regulated by Roman roads and camps. All the forces were in favour of Rome be-

coming not only provincial but even barbarous. And even
Rome itself did to some extent become barbarous. One
small fact, out of many that might be given, may serve to
illustrate a relative condition now so hard to imagine.
When the later disputes arose between the Western Pope
and the Eastern Patriarchs, one of the latter Greek doctors
(if I remember right, the Patriarch of Antioch) offered
himself in a very noble Christian spirit as a peace-maker,
and tried to induce the other Patriarchs to treat the old
Roman priests with respect. And the argument he used
was, almost in these words: "You must not be angry with
the poor Romans; they are rude and ignorant and have
never had our advantages; it is not as if you were argu-
ing with educated people." That is how the merely cultural and social relations stood. And all the time, there
was something underneath; something that was neither
cultural nor social; something that never ceased to repeat, with stubborn and almost sulky repetition, the name
of Peter. And even as morning, noon and night the
brazen and the golden trumpets gave forth to the four
corners of the world the unchallenged proclamation,
"Ubi Cæsar, Ibi Imperium," there came out of the deserted town and the deep places, deep as the dungeon of
the chains, the unvarying answer, "Ubi Petrus, Ibi Ec-
clesia."

But as time went on, something began to be seen in
Constantinople that had never been foreseen by Constantine. Something took hold of the New Rome which

would never perhaps have taken hold of the Old Rome.
Old Rome had been weakened by Asiatic luxuries and
sometimes inflamed by Asiatic sects; but there was something behind these superficial things, something that the
old Roman would never have understood; things more
intangible and more terrible and perhaps more evil,
which can only be called Asiatic abstractions. The
Roman, whatever else he was, had never been a nihilist;
and there was something of nihilism in the night of
mysticism which covered some of the Eastern mystics.
The creed of Mani and Zoroaster was not the particular
sort of Persian apparatus which Horace had ever had
occasion to dispense with. But it was in some ways a
very scientific apparatus; and systems of this rather hard
and inhuman sort were already pressing upon the Eastern frontiers of the Empire and the Church. Perhaps
this tendency can now be seen best in the convention and
compromise in the Greek Orthodox system, by which
an ikon may be a flat picture but must not be a solid
sculpture in the round; and the rather quaint effect of
this compromise, according to which the halo or nimbus,
supposed to be merely a space of light or a ring of fire,
can be carved so as to stand out in solid golden horns and
hoops, more prominent than any human features, while
the human featured face has to remain as flat as a shadow
and as superficial as a diagram. Whatever the reasons
given, or even the contributory causes operating, we can
all feel in this the presence of a certain spirit; awful and

negative and not without grandeur; the Greek in the last days flattening the faces of his gods. For indeed this strange story had a stranger culmination and sequel. It was out of this Byzantine temple, as out of some purely Moslem mosque, that there burst a few centuries later the fury of the Iconoclasts. It is indeed a weird ending to one of the most wonderful stories of history. It was finally the Greeks who went forth to destroy all the statues of the world.

In the path of this whirlwind of fanaticism stood Old Rome ruined and the Pope. He had never in theory lost the power to protest or even to condemn. I can here only roughly summarize a story complicated with endless controversies; but it is true to say that the neglect or desertion of the Roman Pontiff had never been anything but practical and political; one might almost say fashionable. In matters of theory and theology, he had never ceased to claim his authority; and in matters of theory and theology nobody had ever, in any clear and convincing way, denied his authority. But his practical position was weak; and the practical position of the great Patriarchs surrounding the golden throne of Cæsar was very strong. They had behind them not only the whole power of the Sacred Emperor, but the resources of rich, ancient and highly civilized lands; they stood for Alexandria of the Greeks and the Egyptians, for Jerusalem of the Jews, for all that could be inherited of the greatness of Babylon and Assyria, of Sidon and Tyre. All this greatness lay to the East; nothing lay to the West but a wilderness of half-civilized Gauls and uncivilized Goths. This is the situation to be understood if we are to appreciate the point, I might say the shock, of what followed.

The sequel of Constantinople was the result of a separate secular Christian State removed from Old Rome of the martyrs and the memories. Exactly what had happened to it is not easy to describe. There pass from time to time over the mind of man certain vast and mighty moods which make the movements of the world; and one of them passed just then over the whole world that was the Byzantine Empire. Perhaps the nearest we can come to striking the note of it is to say that it was the same movement, of which the complete and conscious and consistent form was the religion of Mahomet. It is an instance of the irony of history that many Byzantine Emperors, who resisted the Moslem invasion with splendid victories or sacrificial deaths, were themselves half Moslems in this deeper movement of the mind. It was rational as the Moslem monotheism is rational. It was fanatical as the Moslem destructiveness was fanatical. It was perhaps something a little like what we call Puritan. But it had more in it of Greek subtlety than Puritanism implies; it was rather as if the Greek genius, which had sought out so many inventions and imaginations, now desired to retire from them and to live only in the mind. It was also affected, as we have seen, by the proximity of the Judaic elements and origins of Christianity. It was

probably affected, more indirectly, by the pessimism and
negation of the Manichees and the mystics of Asia. Much
of it seemed logical enough; but I fancy it is not unfair
to say that Eastern Christianity was a little too Eastern
to be quite Christian. Considering the sense always given
to the antithesis of Hebraism and Hellenism, it is odd
that the end of the Empire that was most Hellenic was
most Hebraic. The stern simplicity of Moses and Mahomet became the ideal of Greeks, the subconscious ideal
even of Catholics; and the quarrel came to an issue over
this matter of whether graven images could be allowed
to Christians. A reaction almost rationalistic had set in
against the idols of paganism, and with it against the
images of Christendom. Perhaps where the Moslem had
a faith, the Christian had only a doubt. But it was a
doubt that hardened more and more into a denial.

Nothing is so hard on the world as the world. Generally, in comparison, there has been much more mercy
and moderation in the Church. Nothing is more inhuman
than humanity itself to human habits, affections or weak-
nesses, when they happen to be unpopular for particular
reasons at a particular moment; and they are likely to be
more ruthlessly treated by a craze than by a creed. Thus
Prohibition was not invented by priests, and is generally
rather opposed by priests. Prohibition was promoted by
a modern political democracy; or rather a plutocracy,
which is still more modern. Very much as the secular
power of a whole continent formally forbade all drinks,

so the secular power of the great Greek Empire formally forbade all dolls or carved images. And Rome refused to join in the old veto as in the new. Just as the Pope would say now that abstinence might be good, but moderation must be innocent, so the Pope said then that images might be abused, but refused to say that they must never be used. Iconoclasm was in the air then, as teetotalism is in the air now; it was the way the world was going and a man might go with it without becoming a Moslem, just as a man can now go with the centralizing sort of social reforms without becoming a Socialist. Men often associated image-breaking with zeal and austerity and the things then most admired; as we associate "temperance reform" with hygiene and science and all the talismanic words of the modern system of magic. It is interesting to note that the Moslem, the real man of that moment, destined to be the conqueror of that epoch and especially of that empire, did actually combine both the ancient and modern veto. Wine as well as statues seemed wicked to him; he was not only as much of an Iconoclast as the Isaurian, but as much of a Prohibitionist as the President of the United States. It is all part of the same mood; and man left to himself is a victim of moods. This mood of prohibition is always a mood of compulsion, of conquest and the cleansing of the earth of every trace of the temporarily detested thing; that sort of man must always crush the human world in order to sift it.

But the Church is not of this world, and can be kinder to it.

Popular history contrasts the Roman with the Greek, and always in one aspect; representing the Greek as graceful and humane but excitable and unstable; the Roman as hard and stolid but orderly and reliable. English writers repeat this so often that they really seem to have forgotten that the Romans were Italians. In fact they sometimes seem to suffer from the illusion that the Romans were Englishmen. In neither case, of course, was the character so simple as that. It would be easy to contradict flatly the legend of the solid Roman and the lively Greek. It would be easy to make a case for the Greek being more harsh and the Roman more amiable. It would be easy to show that the abstract beauty of Greek statues is the beauty of blind and cruel gods; and that, in comparison, the portrait busts that abound in Old Rome are as human and humorous and kindly as a row of portraits by Raeburn or Reynolds. It would be easy to point out that even that early Roman history, represented as so rigid, is really as full of gestures as a gesticulating Italian organ-grinder. It was surely an Italian who shook his robe angrily against the jeering crowd of Tarentum; an Italian who thrust his right hand furiously into the fire of Lars Porsena; an Italian who swore on the uplifted sword a great vengeance on the tribe of Tarquin; an Italian who hurled the head of Hasdrubal into the camp of the Carthaginians. We might add that, while men forget that the Romans were Italians, they also rather curiously forget that the Spartans were Greeks. The theory and practice of Lacedæmon was far more harsh and inhuman than anything in the most savage days of Rome back to the very lair of the wolf. But this method tends to a superficial and special pleading; and the truth is more deep and therefore more delicate. So far as I can guess at it, the truth is this. Both Greeks and Romans were peoples with something in them that seems, by a northern comparison, at once ardent and radiant. They had a store of heat and light, which they used both well and ill. But there was something in the Greeks whereby the rays always struck outwards at some ideal or art or science or object of curiosity. But the Roman radiated inwards, so to speak; he was most himself when he turned back to some interior and intimate relation; his religion was fundamentally domestic; his gods were household gods. Therefore he believed profoundly in modesty and in dignity; and therefore he did seem rigid and respectable compared with a company of Greeks running naked after beauty and philosophy. And this domestic warmth can still be seen in the warm Italian character; and naturally in none more than in the religious, even when they appear to have forsworn domesticity. Nuns are not mothers, but they never seem to be unmotherly. And there were always Vestal Virgins in Rome; but what they guarded was a flame.

Now I think it is true that, as compared with this, the

abstract artistic Greek spirit had something hard about it. In one aspect, there was almost as much that was hard about the Republic of Plato in ideal as about the Republic of Lycurgus in reality. It was frigid in the sense that some found something frigid in Fabianism and the social ideal of Mr. Bernard Shaw. For Bernard Shaw is sometimes as stern as Plato, just as Plato was sometimes as flippant as Bernard Shaw. Similarly, the brutality of the Spartan was not domestic and rustic, like the brutality of Brutus. It was a scientific and sociological brutality, like that of those who would model the state on a beehive or an anthill. The Ideal was the curse of Hellas; for the ideal can be more hardening or even more brutalizing than the real. The Roman mother and child, huddled under the rude wooden Lar, were very real; but Plato dealt with babies in batches like the statisticians of Birth-Control. None of these generalizations, or rather guesses, can cover the field or the many exceptions. But when we remember that the great poet Plato (as he must be called) banished poets from his Republic, we have a glimmer of why the great Greek Emperor banished sculptors from his Empire.

As Hellas when heathen had wished its philosophers to be entirely philosophical, so Hellas turned Christian wished its theologians to be entirely theological. Something at once strict and subtle in its intelligence made all its dialectics as intangible as mathematics. It was as if the world was to be saved rather by the figures of

Euclid than by the figures of Phidias; but chiefly by that sort of Super-Euclid in which there can be no figures at all. The Greek intellect in its last days, in what is loosely called its decline, worked miracles of mental arithmetic in moral and religious matters; it produced definitions and distinctions that are quite as much the masterpieces of their kind as is the Parthenon or the Pindaric Odes. It split hairs quite as perfectly as it had sculptured heroes; but it no longer desired to sculpture heroes. But in Italy there had long been a ruder but a much more rooted tradition both of sculpture and of hero-worship. Only the point was, as I have said, that most of the hero-worship was home-worship. There was therefore in any case something ancestrally and antecedently appropriate about the fact that the Pontifex Maximus stood up for the Western traditions, which had been human even when they were heathen; and in that dark day of invasion the bridge-builder defended the bridge. It was Italy of the household gods that was given up to the fury of the Iconoclasts. Only those household gods had now taken on a new meaning, and with it a new mystery; they were no longer the fables of infancy but the truths of the true religion, calling to the manhood of the world; and that is why it is worth recalling here how the priest by the little town of the Tiber played the part of a man. Christ and Mary had become the greatest of Household Gods. For the West also had to make its contribution to universal religion; they say the East is the home of religions; but in the West is the religion of the home. This is what we must realize if we are to realize the rather dramatic turn of the second great emergence of the Italian spirit. We might almost call it the second rise of Rome against the predominance of Greece. As the doctrinal differences deepened between the Pope and the Patriarchs, they came of course upon other and more theoretical differences than that between the icons of Greece and the statues of Italy. The tremendous and tragic scruple upon the *Filioque* became the formal issue of controversy, along with other matters that now seem rather disproportionate to the disaster of schism; such as the temporary habit of the Westerns of fasting on Saturday; a point on which there is now no longer any difference at all. But I take this quarrel about idolatry, and the affair of the Iconoclasts, partly because it is profoundly typical of the two spirits at work; partly because it is easier to handle as a popular parable turning on a practical action; and partly because I think it had huge historical consequences that have been rather neglected even by the great historians. At the time I speak of, at any rate, the situation was this: The Master of the World, the King of Kings whom even the Christian revolution had hardly made to seem less than a god, leaned his imperial sympathy and protection to this new and naked Hebraism in the East; and supported the new Puritans against the Papacy. It was with Cæsar and civilization behind them that these men went forth to break the Italian statues, as if they were idols of some barbarous Asiatic borderland condemned by a Caliph of Islam.

A man writing these words in Rome stops almost with a start; and looks around him. He sits in a city crowded with churches, with every church crowded with statues. The streets are blocked with fountains wreathed with Tritons and columns surmounted by saints. But it is especially in the great churches designed like classical temples that we have that exuberance of classical realism which possesses everything except classical repose. To some, especially those who love the Northern mysticism of the Gothic, there is something positively oppressive, even repulsive, and as it were indigestible, about these tumultuous and multitudinous marbles; a white nightmare of waving arms and fluttering draperies; something that is cold and colourless and yet boiling and bubbling like one of its own fountains. I have known men who came to hate it so much that it seemed as if the city were plague-stricken with a white leprosy of marble; with the figures of giant lepers writhing and crying out as if possessed. But these men were narrow and nearly mad; and it is worth noting that those who hate the classical revival quite so much as this are generally mediævalists but not Catholics. The Catholic becomes a little more Catholic. The fair way of stating it is that the Renaissance overdid it, as most things overdo themselves; and the things it did are too big to be a detail, too energetic to be a background, and too recent to be a ruin. But these things are largely a matter of mood; and a more masculine mood may yet recover the appetite of our fathers for the stony athletics of these leaping saints and dancing apostles. Whatever they are, the sculptor has made them Muscular Christians. The point here, however, is the strange contrast between Rome Christian and Catholic, as it has come to be to-day, in the course of history, and the mood of that feud of the image-breakers in the Dark Ages. Many a man to-day has felt that there are rather too many statues in Rome. Many a meek tourist may have been tempted to be an Iconoclast. The feeling was stronger about thirty years ago, when Nonconformist tutors and schoolmasters went about carrying Ruskin instead of Baedeker. But that, it might fairly be said, only proved that the statues of the sixteenth century might be more alive than the men of the nineteenth. Anyhow, this prodigious outcrop of sculpture, which some think heathen and which is certainly very human, was in history the crown of Christian Rome and the final flowering of the power of the Papacy. And it is curious to remember that in those first dim days it hung on this one thread of a theological distinction in the disputes of the Dark Ages.*

Theological distinctions are fine but not thin. In all the mess of modern thoughtlessness, that still calls itself

* The distinctions were so fine, and even faint, that I am forced here to shorten and simplify a most complex story. I envy and admire Mr. Wells. Everybody wavered under the wind of Iconoclasm; but the Western Church stiffened against it—and so produced Statues and the Renaissance.

modern thought, there is perhaps nothing so stupendously stupid as the common saying, "Religion can never depend on minute disputes about doctrine." It is like saying that life can never depend on minute disputes about medicine. The man who is content to say, "We do not want theologians splitting hairs," will doubtless be content to go on and say, "We do not want surgeons splitting filaments more delicate than hairs." It is the fact that many a man would be dead to-day, if his doctors had not debated fine shades about doctoring. It is also the fact that European civilization would be dead to-day, if its doctors of divinity had not debated fine shades about doctrine. Nobody will ever write a History of Europe that will make any sort of sense, until he does justice to the Councils of the Church, those vast and yet subtle collaborations for thrashing out a thousand thoughts to find the true thought of the Church. The great religious Councils are far more practical and important than the great international treaties, which are generally made the pivotal dates of history. Our everyday affairs at this moment are far more affected by Nicæa and Ephesus and Basle and Trent than they are by Utrecht or Amiens or Vienna or Versailles. For in almost every case, the international peace was founded on a compromise; the religious peace was founded on a distinction. It was not a compromise to say that Jesus Christ was Perfect God and Perfect Man; as it was a compromise to say that Danzig should be partly Polish and partly German. It was the enunciation of a principle, of which the very completeness distinguishes it from the Monophysite on the one side and the Arian on the other. And it has affected, and does still affect, the general state of mind of thousands of Europeans, from admirals to apple-women, who do think (even vaguely) of Christ as something human and divine. To ask the apple-woman what are the present practical results for her of the Treaty of Utrecht would be less than fruitful. Now our civilization is simply made up of these old moral decisions; which many think minute decisions. On the day which ended certain metaphysical disputations about Fate and Freedom, it was decided whether Austria should look like Arabia; or whether travelling in Spain should be the same as travelling in Morocco. When the dogmatists drew a fine distinction between the sort of honour due to marriage and the sort of honour due to virginity, they stamped the culture of a whole continent with a definite pattern of red and white; a pattern which some people may not like; but which all people recognize when they revile. When men distinguished between lawful lending and usury, they created an actual historical human conscience, which even the enormous modern triumph of usury, in the materialistic age, has not yet wholly destroyed. When St. Thomas Aquinas defined true property, and also defined the abuses of false property, the tradition of that truth made a real recognizable breed of men, to be recognized to-day in the mob politics of Melbourne or Chicago; almost always differing from the Communists in admitting property; yet almost always in practice in protest against plutocracy. In short, these thin distinctions grew up into very thick and thorough-going principles and even prejudices. If such a theological distinction is a thread, all Western history has hung on that thread; if it is a fine point, all our past has been balanced on that point. The subtle distinctions have made the simple Christians; all the men who think drink right and drunkenness wrong; all the men who think marriage normal and polygamy abnormal; all the men who think it wrong to hit first and right to hit back; and, as in the present case, all the men who think it right to carve statues and wrong to worship them. These are all, when one comes to think of it, very subtle theological distinctions.

But the case of the statues has a special importance in the argument here. It is true, as I have said, that many of these, the finest and the most fruitful distinctions, have been made by the recognized Councils; by those armies of sacred diplomatists drawing up the Treaties of Truth, or at least the Truces of God. But the same fact is even more striking when the whole future depended upon a single distinction and the single distinction depended upon a single man. Whatever the reader may think, in a theological sense, about the function claimed by the Pope, in relation to the functions of the Council, as of the Bible or any other authority, he should have enough his-

torical imagination to feel that there was something his-
torically momentous about that lonely man and that large
and spreading destiny. It was the Pope alone, for all practical purposes, who stood out upon the fine distinction
between imagery and idolatry. It was the Pope alone,
therefore, who prevented the whole artistic area of
Europe, and even the whole map of the modern world,
from being as flat and featureless as a Turkey carpet.
Indeed we may well compare it to a Turkey carpet; for
it would soon have been a carpet for the Turks.

May I pause here to say to the impatient that many
people visiting Rome might just as well have visited Rat-
cliff Highway, because they will not stop to consider historical stories of this kind? They themselves may happen
to be without a theology, or even without a religion. So
I am myself, I deeply and bitterly regret to say, without
a mythology. Nothing would give me greater pleasure
than to possess a nice complicated pagan mythology. But
if I were studying the shrines of pagan mythology, I
should not complain because it was complicated. Living
Rome was built upon theology; as much as dead Rome
was built upon mythology. Nobody can understand dead
Rome, or even dead Pompeii, without some familiarity
with the branching fictions and fantastic pedigrees of
gods and demigods in whom he does not believe. Whatever his opinions may be, surely he need not avoid the
legends of living Rome merely because they are still
living. And unless he tries to understand the moral and

mystical principles, thousands of years old, which are the roots of the living Rome, he will make no sense of its flowers of sculpture and decoration; and least of all where the flowers are a little florid.

In those days there was no question, of course, of such sculpture in that emptied and provincialized Italy. I suppose it was a matter of a few archaic dolls; stiff and naïve images that might be thought suitable to nurseries rather than shrines. But all things begin in the mind; and that Pope was defending Donatello's George and Michael Angelo's Moses; and because he stood firm in Rome the great David stands gigantic over Florence and the little Della Robbias have crept like scraps of sky and cloud into the palace of Perugia and the cells of Assisi. He was saving something destined to be a sign and a splendour and, most valuable of all, a scandal. The wholly humanized emblem of humanity, the figure in the round, was indeed to become the test and the standard and the stumbling-block by which our enemies know us and we know ourselves. And if the images were then, and if they sometimes still are, like dolls meant for children, that also is an allegory and one not without authority. Even in this story of a remote pontiff and his statues it is not irrelevant; for he called on children to defend them.

To read the riddle of Rome in that hour we must strip it of all these rich accumulations of its policy; we must dismiss or dispel all this mob of marble figures, all this white cloud of witnesses to its patronage of art and antiquity; we must see it as the little walled Italian town it must have seemed in the seventh century, with bare brick or meagre Byzantine mosaic, and beyond it, as the traveller went northward, less and less of even that limited culture to lift the villages or break the line of the hills. Beyond the Alps were the hardly won conquests of Cæsar; beyond the Rhine was the formless world of forests which even Cæsar had hardly condescended to conquer. And from those forests, and across that river, were now trickling a thin stream of tribes; men from the ends of the earth to be an omen of the end of the world. Heavy hairy men, who had never known even the outlandish Celtic culture of Britain and Gaul, waded the fords and crawled across the fields; and found the Roman road and took even the island town of Lutetia. Some of these were called Franks and, though few in number, somehow gave their name to the land; they became Christians in some fashion and of one of their savage kings the noble story is told, that when he heard the tale of the Crucifixion, he grasped his rude weapons and cried, "Had I been there with my Franks!" Broadly, however, he and his like came from a barbarous world into a half-barbarous world; and had no more notion than their own cattle of the questions that were debated by the Greeks and the Italians under Byzantine arches or Egyptian obelisks. The great hills that hung over Italy like thunder-clouds were, after all, the outposts of an outer world of stormy savagery and gloom. And to these hills the High Pontiff lifted up his eyes; the hills from whence came his help.

In a momentous hour, weighted not only with the doom but I think with the very existence of all of us, in an hour which so changed the balance of the world that without it we should not have been, the Pope began a new policy. He attempted the paradox of a new orientation away from the orient. In that hour he turned his back upon the sun; upon the sunrise and all the light and learning that was associated with the sunny lands; now in the possession of some mad Manichæan autocracy. He appealed to the uncivilized against the overcivilized; he even appealed to the unconverted against the relapsed. With this occasion there begins most clearly the very common Papal policy of appealing to friends who were far off against enemies who were near. The Father of Christendom decided to awaken the West. He decided to raise up the new and as yet nameless nations; to raise up France and Britain; to raise up you and me. He troubled the waters of those vast stagnant inland pools; he stirred up the mud and started the stream that was to be our own story; he began the movement which was to make our Western Europe the head of the world. Without the religious element, in the curious interlude that followed, I see no reason to doubt that Goths would have gone on being Goths to the crack of doom, as Red Indians went on being Red Indians to the coming of Columbus. The North had indeed been planted out to some extent with monasteries and missions that maintained the Catholic name; but they were perpetually being washed away again by heathen invasions; they would hardly have played the first part in the world but for the fact that followed. The fact was that the Pope began to make a new Roman Empire. In the phrase invented for a smaller matter fifteen hundred years later, he did, if ever a man did, call in the New World to redress the balance of the Old.

The first stage of the story concerned this business of the Iconoclasts. When those fanatics landed in Italy to destroy the Italian images, they found themselves confronted with new and outlandish men from the North; the Franks who had already crossed the Alps as they had crossed the Rhine. In the battles that followed the breaking of the image-breakers was at least as vigorous as their own breaking of the images; and of this particular fever of fanaticism Italy was soon swept free. But it was the beginning of a policy and the end of that policy was far more important and impressive. The King of the Franks, however little he may have understood of the help he was giving, was not a man without Latin and civilized connections; and the son he left behind him was in practice a Gaul who was more than half a Roman. He was also one of the most remarkable men in the history of the world.

Not very long after the great Greek Emperor, Leo the Isaurian, had issued a universal proclamation, commanding every single subject in the whole Roman Empire to swear to his hatred of images and his acceptance of Iconoclasm, Pope Gregory III rose up and excommunicated the Iconoclasts. The Emperor called a Council of the Church which supported the imperial view. The Pope condemned the Council. It would be impossible to bring into sharper outline and conflict the claims of the two powers. But in practice, those who knew them to be incompatible felt them to be incommensurate. It is impossible, as I have said, to recreate after all these ages and alterations, the huge disproportion that seemed to exist between the broad daylight of the Empire and the faint shadow in the West. I have compared it to Winchester challenging London; it was more as if the York diocese defied the modern financial position of New York. New Rome seemed as prosperous and promising as New York. It seemed as central and civilized as Paris. It seemed as natural a seat of new experiments as the real New Rome of to-day. The Emperor had on his side councils and colleges and the bishops of big cities and the whole tone and talk of society and the prestige of the past and the promise of the future. The Pope had on his side deserted streets and barren provinces and frontiers broken by barbarians and the support of rude and uncertain tribes; the Pope had on his side savagery and stupidity and ignorance and desolation; and the Pope was right.

He was right thoroughly; he was right a thousand times; he was right by the creative Christian principle, in which the devil cannot make but only mar; he was right equally by every modern test or taste in beauty and the liberty of the arts; he was right against the Cæsarean fad of flat portraits as much as against the Moslem mono-mania of monotheism; he was right by the whole power and spirit of the wide culture that was already dawning darkly behind; he was as right as the oldest gargoyle of Chartres or the last statuette of Cellini; he was right with the unconscious prophecy of all that has here covered him with the flamboyance and the splendour of Rome; and he was right when every one else was wrong. Realize only that one forgotten fact about that one ob-scure Pontiff; and then come back to consider afresh, with what detachment and independence you will, the impression that at first puzzled you; the impression that this temple of St. Peter is built to assert rather the firm-ness and authority and even audacity of its hierarchs than their softness or simplicity or sympathy as holy men. Realize that for many millions of mankind, including those who made this city and this shrine, it is really true; the same thing that happened in the matter of the Icono-clasts has happened again and again; and in the awful silence after some shattering question, one voice has spoken and one signal has saved the world. Never mind whether you believe this or not; fully and fairly realize that they believe it; and *then* for the first time you will be at the beginning of all comprehension of such a statuary and such a dome. You will begin to know what

[71]

is all that any art critic needs to know; what the artist is driving at; and why he drove in this direction and not in that. You will understand why the building is almost oppressive in its hanging curves, almost homeless in its vast and glimmering floors, why so many dead Popes seem to hang above us thunderously like judges or point suddenly like accusers. For this is not the place where we come nearest to the charity and burning tenderness of the Heart of Christ; we can come far nearer on the gaunt and arid rocks of Assisi. For the rocks of Nature are gentle compared with the rocks of Michael Angelo. This is not the place specially designed to express that element of twilight and a reverent doubt, the spirit which at once accepts the mystery and gives up the riddle. That is far better conveyed in many grey vistas of the Gothic, following in their very tracery the long winters and uncertain skies of the north. What the architect or sculptor was driving at here, what he was set to do and finally and magnificently did, was to carve something that should in some dim degree express the Certitude of Rome. The Popes are not here laid prostrate with folded hands, in the more pious mediæval manner, because religious art in this phase is not thinking of them as men now peacefully dead, but as men who on this or that occasion were terribly alive. It is thinking of them as orators who spoke certain words, as judges who made certain decisions, like that one decision I have already noted as the origin of all such massive and many-sided sculpture. The motto emblazoned round the great dome is not, as a very thoughtful Unitarian once complained that it should be, the words of Peter acknowledging Christ; but the words of Christ establishing Peter. But this is all in the same line of purpose, when once we have understood the purpose. There are places and shrines enough, thank God, in which all people, Popes and all, can testify to their infinite insignificance in the presence of Jesus Christ. But this is the particular place where is to be asserted, rightly or wrongly, the certitude of a certain person or persons that they do in deadly fact possess a special warrant from Him. This is where the *claim* is made; with trumpets and under a banner as in a mediæval castle. The scroll that surrounds the dome *is* flamboyant, for it is a flame; it is defiant, for it is a banner; it is sensational, for it is a proclamation to the whole people. Once get these two ideas of Certitude and the Spoken Word into your mind, and you will begin to understand St. Peter's, even if you never like it. No case of the Spoken Word could be clearer than this I have chosen; where the Pope upheld the sculptors against the Empire and the world. No place could equal St. Peter's as showing how confidently and audaciously men went forward in that word.

Because of his single word the Statue stands central and erect in Christendom; the type of reality; facing all ways and to be seen from every side. The flat face of the Oriental ikon is really by comparison that of a ghost.

For it is in a special sense an appearance; which is also called an apparition. Seen aslant, from another standpoint, it is distorted or disappears. A picture may in a true sense be a vision, but it is still in one sense an illusion; when we pass behind it, it is gone. And this is truly a type of something much deeper in the doctrine of the ikons; we might say something much deeper in their shallowness. There was something in it of that hollow and heartless mysticism which the Pope and his predecessors had felt in the earlier heresies. Between him and them was all that deep quarrel with the Gnostics and those who held that Christ had indeed gone about like a shining shadow, that his appearances were only apparitions; and even that a horrible wraith or hallucination had hung and cried upon the Cross. Behind it was all that evil purity and unearthly refinement that were so much more blasphemous than the manly materialism of St. Thomas, which Christ honoured with a proof. A profound Christian instinct made the early Popes bury all such visionaries like vampires; and set up on their graves this pillar of sanity, the Statue, something as solid as it is stupendous.

They speak more truly than they know who say that the sign and scandal of the Catholic Church is the Graven Image. The Church forbids us to worship it save as a symbol; but as a symbol it is most solidly symbolic. For it stands for this strange mania of Certitude, without which Rome will remain a riddle; it stands for the intolerant and intolerable notion that something is really true; true in every aspect and from every angle; true from the four quarters of the sky; true by the three dimensions of the Trinity. We turn from it and it does not vanish; we analyze it and it does not dissolve; at last, after long and laborious experiments in scepticism, we are forced to believe our eyes.

III · THE PILLAR OF THE LATERAN

There is a sense in which the highest object of historical learning is to unlearn history. At least, it is the object to unthink it or unimagine it. The point is what is called a paradox; but it is one well worth pointing out. We do not realize what the past has been until we also realize what it might have been. We are merely imprisoned and narrowed by the past, so long as we think that it must have been. For that is only the provincial presumption that it must have been what it was because it had to produce what it did; that is, our own precious and priceless selves. It is difficult for us to believe that the huge human thing called history might actually have taken another turn and done without us. The most pathetic part of it is that it would never have known what it had lost. Mr. Brown of Brixton has been taught to call himself the Heir of All the Ages; but, as a mere matter of detail, the Ages never made any last will and testament actually mentioning Mr. Brown. There is far more philosophy, to my mind, in what seems to some the fantastic speculations of the mediæval Schoolmen, when they argue for pages about what would have happened to the plants or the planets if Adam had never eaten the apple. They at least had the immense and mighty imagination of which I speak; they could unthink the past. They could uncreate the Fall. With a reverence which moderns might think impudence, they could uncreate the Creation.

In other words, we must say first to the historical student, not only "Where were you when the foundations of the world were laid?" but "Where would you be, if anywhere, if the foundations had been laid a little differently?" And this applies not only to absolute foundations like the Creation or the Fall, but to the main foundation-stones of secular history such as the Roman Empire or the Reformation. We have to stretch our minds to conceive a world in which Rome had never come westward, let alone touched the Atlantic isles, or in which England were still as Papist as Ireland. Until we can retrospectively remove these enormous things, as if they were enormous obstacles, we cannot even really understand the difference they have made to the landscape. The historian needs a destructive imagination as well as a creative one; even in order to create. He must have the imagination to unimagine. Otherwise, the mere necessitarian will always be narrow; for such a man will really be working upon the insane notion, or obsession, that he is necessary.

It is the root of all religion that a man knows that he is nothing in order to thank God that he is something.

In the same way the human race, like the human being, does not really appear out of the abyss until we have in the abstract abolished it. Until we can fancy that the great human events did not happen, we cannot really feel that they did happen. So long as we only take them for granted we do not take them at all; and certainly do not take them in their enormity and entirety. We must realize that, in the mind at least, Athens might never have been built, the Jews might have been exterminated in the first fight with the Canaanites, all Europe might have become Moslem or no civilization existed except the Chinese. I am sure that the right way to the realization of history is through this sort of imaginative destruction; but when it comes to the case before me, and I consider that it is ourselves and all our own history that has thus to be imaginatively destroyed, I despair.

In short, we forget the hinges of history, and above all, that hinges move freely. "For all we have and are," as somebody said, I fear in a more limited connection. Most vividly and literally, for all we have and are, we are indebted to that dark hour in the very midnight of the Dark Ages, when Rome, under the rule of the Popes, turned for the second time towards the West. Rome was not now overpowering the West with her strength, but rather calling upon the West in her weakness. Rome was not sending forth legions like Cæsar; she was rather borrowing or drawing down legions from Charlemagne. But because she was Christian Rome and no longer Pagan

Rome she was not afraid of the paradox; and verified the maxim that the weak things of the earth will confound the strong. For what actually followed on that appeal of the Pope to the Franks is an episode so extraordinary, so symbolic, so determining and at the same time so mysterious and apparently so brief, that all subsequent centuries have in some fashion remained staring at it. But it was certainly one of the most practical and productive things in Christian history; and it became almost more practical by changing from history to legend.

I suppose every sensible person, unsophisticated by Nordic nonsense, can see the obvious fact that Rome originally civilized the North and that otherwise it would have remained uncivilized. Otherwise the North Sea Islands would have been pretty much like the South Sea Islands. In that sense Julius Cæsar was as adventurous, and almost as accidental a discoverer as Captain Cook. It is less self-evident, but it seems to me pretty clear, that the North would have been lost again to civilization, and much of the West as well, when the Cæsars of the last days so resolutely marched eastward for their Empire. It was saved by the fact that the Popes did not march eastward with the Cæsars. It was especially saved by the fact that the Popes came at last to defy their Eastern Cæsars; and it was saved most of all by the fact that the Popes finally dared to set up Cæsars of their own. That they came at last to quarrel with their Western, as they had quarrelled with their Eastern, emperors was but an example

of their permanent policy of being independent of any
earthly power when it was really powerful. But it was not
until centuries afterwards that the new Holy Roman
Empire was in any final sense very powerful; and the
miracle of the renewal of hope in the very moment of
the worst Western decline belongs rather to a manifestation which was, in the immediate sense, as broken and
brief as it was splendid. But it made such a difference
that men were never able afterwards to express the difference it made; and had to suggest it somehow in symbol
and poetry.

It is when a fact is thus too big for history that it over-
flows the surrounding facts and expresses itself in fable.
Nay, it is when the fact is in a sense too solid that its
very solidity breaks the framework of ordinary things;
and it can only be recorded through extraordinary things
like fairy-tales and romances of chivalry. Everybody felt
that merely saying that one Carolus or Carl had lived
and died at a certain date, and had a palace at Aix, and
fought such and such campaigns against Saxons or Sara-
cens, was wholly inadequate to explain what had happened. Nothing short of saying that Charlemagne was ten
feet high, or that he lived for two hundred years, was at
all upon the scale of what had happened. For what had
happened was that in the dead and deserted lands on
which the world had turned its back, in the densest and
blindest forests of relapsing ignorance and decay, there
had come a vision; a vision of light and loyalty and order

or the wild possibility of these things; white against the darkness, the face of a great king; a face never to be forgotten. It is impossible to describe, or perhaps even to conjecture, exactly how these things affect mankind. Wherever they occur, they become the legends that are larger than history. Such has been the tradition of King Arthur in Britain. Such has been the tradition of St. Patrick in Ireland. But these great men were in their time inevitably more localized; they were not in a central position to represent the whole world, like an Emperor crowned by a Pope. Yet this had happened relatively at the ends of the earth where no man expected it. It may be compared to a miracle if only by a metaphor. For it was a Sunrise in the West.

Men had to imagine Charlemagne; it was inadequate merely to record him. But being imagined is not the same as being imaginary. It is sometimes the wildest effort of imagination for a man to imagine what he actually sees. But in historical retrospect the paradox I have noted remains. In order to imagine him, we have first to unimagine him. We have to realize the difference that his disappearance from history would have made. I believe myself that, but for this episode, our Western world would at best have developed quite differently, and most probably not developed at all. From the Carolingian episode comes the whole of that conception of Chivalry, which has become the secular morality of the West; and a thousand times more so because the glory from which it comes is not only glory but in some sense defeat. Chivalry is in itself a new and Christian view of defeat. Charlemagne, like Arthur, owes his everlasting success to the fact that he did not succeed. He did not heal the barbarian wounds of the West, but he showed men a sort of hope of their being healed. In the story of Roland, and in all the stories since derived from that origin, there is exactly the same secret of defeat that is not despair. To tell the tale of how that idea flowered and unfolded would simply be to tell the story of Gaul and Britain and Spain and all the rest from the night of the ninth century to the present hour. But the immediate interest of the matter for me, and the reason why I have dwelt upon it here, is the curious coincidence of its origin. It all really began with that old stubborn priest beside the Tiber, and the rally of the Roman authority against the Byzantine power. It began, as much as anywhere, in that squabble of the fanatics from Asia Minor declaring war upon the statues of Italy. It was the Italian instinct, as well as the Papal authority, that felt itself at that moment the defender of solid and human and reasonable things, and knew that the zeal of the Isaurian was a wind from the desert and not only a light from the dawn.

We have seen that Byzantium endeavoured to reduce Rome to a provincial town; and that Rome refused to be provincial, and roused herself once again to be imperial. But in this first of the Roman revivals touched upon here, she became imperial in a rather new and revolutionary fashion. Instead of trying to continue the line of local Cæsars, when it had died out, she had looked frankly westward for an Emperor of the West; thereby doing what she has more than once done, as even this rough outline would indicate: meeting the immediate need of the time, in the largest and boldest spirit, but laying up other troubles for other times, to be taken in turn as they came. The Popes preferred the risk of crowning a barbarian Cæsar to the risk of bowing down before a Byzantine one. Fortunately, in the principal case, the barbarian was not a barbarian. He was not only a genius but a man of mainly Gallic origin and Roman culture; but he was near enough to the barbarians to have been turned into a German after he was dead. When this idea of a Western Emperor reappeared in the West, it had really and truly become a German thing; and the Popes seem to have felt something vaguely barbaric about it, in spite of the distinction of many of its individual princes. Anyhow, there followed that long war in the West between Pope and Emperor which is the next great phase in the history of Rome. It may be remarked that the history of Rome, between the death and relative failure of Charlemagne and the rise of those who claimed to be his successors, was an interlude of deep depression and degradation. It was the ninth century, the midnight of the Dark Ages; the North and West was swallowed as if in a sea-mist by the Danish raiders from the sea, and would probably never have reappeared but for two things; the gallant defence of Paris and the heroic pertinacity of Alfred the Great.

But these heroes were at the outposts. There were precious few heroes in the high places of Christendom. The palace revolutions of the Papacy seemed subject to mere barbarian caprice; and puppets were put up and pulled down for the sport of almost savage princes. There were Popes who were mere boys, yet who managed to gain the reputation of matured blackguards. There never was a moment when Christian civilization seemed so obviously at the very moment of dissolution, as in this dim distraction of the ninth century; yet here also Rome and the Papacy weathered the storm and all the scandals only accumulated to be swept away in the next of the great Roman resurrections; when there arose towering above the Church, in the first twilight of the true Middle Ages, the greatness of Gregory the Seventh.

Hildebrand, the hammer of the Simonists and the false and venal priests of his time, was in his own person an embodiment of this recurring theme of the Resurrection of Rome. The disputes about him rather resemble those about Mussolini; for in the same way, a modern man may disapprove some of his sweeping reforms, and approve others; but finds it difficult not to admire even where he does not approve. His two great campaigns, of course, were that against the corruption and anarchy of ecclesiastical discipline and that against the secular power of the German Cæsars. Many Catholics who

approve the first as necessary criticize the second as excessive; but I think he was a thousand times right to refuse
the secular domination of the German Emperor, as his
forebears had refused that of the Greek Emperor. Anyhow, he himself had certainly no doubts about it; there
never was a man who was more all of a piece; and from
his first peasant beginnings to his death in a strange land,
everything he did or said had a sound like iron. I know
nothing finer in its way than his last bold piece of irony
and even parody of Scripture: "I have loved justice and
hated iniquity; therefore I die in exile."

So far as I have any right to an opinion on so tangled
a story, my own politics are entirely Guelph. I think
it was a visible divine blessing upon the Papal policy
that most of the wealth and grandeur and the great
feudal aristocracy was on the other side. There was of
course any amount of ambition and general anarchy and
wickedness on both sides. But on the whole the Popes
were on the side of the people; of the little republics;
of the cities where men were citizens. I know that Dante
was a Ghibelline politician,* and I think he was a good
deal too free with his hell-fire in the support of his own
particular brand of politics. Doubtless there was a great
deal to be said for his great vision of the double empire
of Cæsar and Peter; but, after all, it had already failed
when Cæsar was a highly cultivated Greek, and I doubt

* I know this is now disputed; at least he was an Imperialist, or more so
than many Guelphs.

if it would have permanently succeeded when the Cæsar was translated into the Kaiser. Certainly Frederick the Second, with all his talents, was a mere enemy of Christendom; much more of an enemy than Mahomet. I hope it is true, as I have seen it stated, that it was really the Emperor Frederick who first began to burn heretics. I should like it to have been invented by an atheist.

Eventually, of course, the feud of the Guelphs and Ghibellines trailed itself into such a tangle that no rational person could trouble any more about it; but by that time the particular phase of the Papacy, which we call the War of the Investitures, had ended in the essential victory of the Pope. As I say, I do not claim to be an authority; but I am glad. I think the Holy Roman Empire might have turned into a very Unholy Roman Empire. And, like the men of the mediæval republics of Italy, I am a Nationalist; and I think it a good thing, on the whole, that Europe, which when Pagan had had one realm and many religions, should when Christian have one religion and many realms.

Rome is too small for its greatness, or too great for its smallness, or whatever the word may be; there is from the first an element of concentration amounting to congestion. Though it seems superficially a city standing in the flattest and most open sort of plain, there is not in fact any sense of that centrifugal spirit we now associate with a city. Everything looks inwards and not outwards; and everything runs down to a centre, even to excess. It

[89]

is partly (as I have said) that a city of seven hills is naturally one of several valleys; and standing on any such
hill, like that of the Pincian Gardens, we have a sense that
the valleys are like chasms; that they are cloven down
into the depths like the canyons of the Western mountains. We feel that the hills, though covered with houses,
are not Rome but rather the walls of Rome; and we are
eternally drawn towards that leap and plunge that proved
fatal to the brother of Romulus. Something in the lines
of that stony landscape is as centripetal as a splendid
whirlpool; and the whole is a movement always return-
ing to its own centres. For that reason there is so much
stratification in the place, and the piling of one period
on another; there is nothing that corresponds to the scattered fringe and litter of little Norman and Gothic
churches through the countrysides of the north. All roads
lead to Rome; and towards the end, they seem in a hurry
to get there. Thus Mediævalism is merely buried in
Rome, as if it were a period like that of the cave-men or
the lake-dwellers. Too much has been piled on top of
it, and in too much of a hurry; and the chief city of antiquity is not even sufficiently antiquated. A platform of
pagan Rome has been preserved, but preserved as a sort
of open-air museum; deliberately preserved as something
dead and detached, with which men have no more to do.
But Christian Rome has crushed Christian Rome, one
vigorous Christian epoch trampling down another, in a
perpetual pagoda of revolution and conquest; indeed

nobody could look at that tower of inventions and novelties without realizing that Christianity has been the religion of revolutions. But the disadvantage of this congestion is that the thing submerged has been submerged
too much. A man need not be a mad mediævalist, or have
a narrow devotion to the narrow and devotional arches
of the Gothic, in order to feel that much of Rome would
be more real if its architecture were less theatrical; and if
some of the things that were significant to St. Catherine
or to Dante had remained as they were; like the cathedral
where Thomas Becket was butchered or the cathedral
where Joan of Arc led the King. I do not know exactly
what was the architecture of St. John Lateran in the
early thirteenth century; not certainly Northern Gothic;
I suppose something more analogous to that of Giotto's
tower; but a man standing before the church would still
like to imagine it toppling like the Tower of Pisa, as it
did in the great Pope's nightmare. It would be possible
of course to imagine the present structure falling; I have
even known fastidious critics who would be glad if it
should fall. But it is not the Church that Innocent and
Francis saw; and there are not enough things in Rome
that are as the mediæval men saw them. It is needless to
add that this sort of creative congestion, or the blocking
of old things with new, is still native to the place and
has gone on into our own time. The great glaring monument of Victor Emmanuel is quite a good piece of work
of its kind, just as the Renaissance temples and foun-

tains are quite good pieces of work of their kind. There is really nothing to be said against it except that it is in the way. It is a bad thing when the mind, called on to criticize any artistic creation, thinks first of an object as an obstacle. That is what has been the matter with Rome for four centuries; too many of the things are obstacles to other things. The recent past has got too much in the way of the remote past; to such an extent that in some cases men must go underground to find it. This is, or may be, a defect; but it is not a defect of death, but rather of a riot and extravagance of resurrection.

The last chapter was largely concerned with St. Peter's; if only as a sort of background for meditation on the primal mystery of the Papacy and the importance of the early Popes. If we considered that matter in the light and shadow of St. Peter's, we might well go on to consider the next historic phase in the second great church of St. John Lateran. In both cases, of course, the environment is suggestive rather than strictly historical. In the concrete sense, naturally, there is nothing Early Christian about St. Peter's except its name and (as some think) its nature. It is pure Renaissance; and for those who find such Renaissance effervescence is merely frothy, St. Peter's dome will only be the very biggest soap-bubble in such a world of froth. Similarly, I shall not blame such a gentleman, with his prejudices, if he finds something rather soapy about St. John Lateran. That also, with some exceptions to be mentioned later, is quite the reverse of a reminder of the next epoch of mediæval Rome. But then there hardly is any reminder of mediæval Rome. And it may seem a somewhat dismal paradox to devote this chapter on Rome to something that cannot be found there.

And yet this classic façade of the Lateran will always be, for some of us, more alive with the Middle Ages than Notre Dame. For it was here that the same Innocent III made momentary contact with that strange man who made or remade the Middle Ages, and whose flaming figure still burns where their brightest colours have grown dark. Francis of Assisi kicked his heels here like a beggar and spoke so as to be mistaken for a madman; but the Pope to whom he had spoken dreamed, it is said, in the watches of the night when sleep had softened the watchful guards of his gigantic common sense, that he saw the whole Mother Church of Christians stooping terribly out of heaven like a deluge of ruin; and only the lean figure of the lunatic upholding it and preventing its fall. It is very likely that Innocent really saw in his dream, without understanding, the secret of the Middle Ages.

It would therefore seem somewhat harder in Rome for the mediæval Popes to rise from the dead; and the excessive concentration of northern culture on Dante has left an exaggerated impression that they would rise from the damned. Yet mediæval civilization was great in Rome as it was great everywhere; and I suppose the supreme mo-

ment of the purely mediæval Papacy might be put somewhere about the time of Innocent III. It is true, of course,
that the mediæval rebirth of civilization could never be
quite so striking in Italy as elsewhere; simply because
what was reborn had never so completely died. Learning and the arts had been more like an aged invalid when
elsewhere they were like a new-born child. Even the
Dark Ages were not so completely dark; Italy was in
the moral what Norway is in the material world. It was
the Land of the Midnight Sun. But if in those southern
cities the sun had never completely set, it gave them in
some ways an emotion of endless evening rather than
morning; and prevented some morning energies of
mediævalism from doing themselves justice. That is why
there is really no good Gothic in Italy. For a long time
the South had only long memories of preservation;
while in the North there were only memories of renewal,
or rather of building which was not even recognized
as rebuilding. So that if we wish to find, in Rome itself,
something suggestive of the greatness of the great age
of Innocent III, we must approach the matter indirectly,
and even look for the reflection of the mediæval in
the modern mind. Innocent III, though but a small temporal prince, towered over the most terrible of the princes
of his day. He mastered like a lion-tamer the lion brood
of the Plantagenet; he defeated in statecraft even the
deep strategy of Philip Augustus, and all the great and
growing power of France; he broke the chain of the

Holy Roman Empire; he was the arbiter of Christendom. Yet if we seek for this great Papal epoch in the Papal city, we are in practice driven to look for it in a later memorial; and in the belated but powerful effect of that epoch upon our own.

There is a silly habit in some travellers of ignoring everything that is Modern. It is especially common among Modernists. It is generally the very people who tell the Church to live up to the lofty standard of the twentieth century, who pride themselves on shutting their eyes to everything she has done after the twelfth. The motive is almost vulgarly obvious. It is simply their way of insinuating that the cult of Jesus Christ passed away at some particular date, like the cult of Jupiter-Ammon. Many methods have been employed for achieving or announcing that destruction; and the world having sent against the sanctuary armies of soldiers with spears and anarchists with torches, has lately sent an army of antiquaries with spades. But even where this bitter and bigoted motive does not exist, there is in any case a curious modern fashion for seeking out only what is old-fashioned. By this limitation the full logic of the story is entirely lost. There is a story of a man who persisted in reading the Greek Testament aloud because he wanted to know what happened to Peter. Nobody who refuses to follow the story to modern times has the least notion of what happened to Peter. The man who only reads the guide-book reads a story that begins without an ending; just as the man who reads only the newspaper reads a story that ends without a beginning. And the Modernist is a man who does, in spirit at least, read only the guide-book at one end and the newspaper at the other. What he misses in between is the gigantic modern development of ancient things; developed in so direct a fashion that, without understanding the ancient, we cannot understand the modern. Treated as an inscription on a tomb, it is an almost undecipherable inscription; and treated as a news item in the newspapers, it is quite meaningless news. What we want is the bridge between the two; and again we find something symbolic in the title of Pontifex, the bridge-builder.

I will take two examples from the Church of St. John Lateran, one of the recognized sites both for pilgrims and for sight-seers. Both these things are modern and there-fore neither of these things is pointed out to modern people; certainly not to tourists and I have my doubts even about pilgrims. Yet one of them stands for the Mediæval world and the other for the Modern world in an aptness of antithesis as plain and pointed as an epi-gram. Nobody who readily neglects the first is really in-terested in the Middle Ages; though he impale himself on pointed arches or is struck "mute" for ever, attitudiniz-ing before Botticelli. Nobody who readily neglects the second really cares a rap about the story of modern times, though he be smothered in newspapers telling him about the patriotism of Mr. Snowden or the spirituality of Mr.

Hoover. They are there in the world-famous Lateran Church; and I doubt whether one man in fifty will even know to which two objects I refer.

It is the more interesting because the Lateran Church is full of interesting objects; but of different sorts that interest different people. I need not describe the only too tempestuous statuary that stands all down the middle; in the last, and possibly the worst, but at least the most boisterous stage of the Baroque. The general impression is that the Twelve Apostles always preferred to stand in a draught, but that they inhabited a curious country where the wind blew in all the opposite ways at once. Perhaps some such licence might be allowed to the supernatural wind of Pentecost, which was truly a wind of liberty in the sense of a wind of isolating individualism; bringing different gifts to different people; a good wind that blew nobody harm. But the actual effect on the senses, in this cold marble corridor, is merely that the bewildered Christians have got into a heathen temple of the winds. All this sort of criticism is trite, but it is true. Moreover, when all allowance is made for a right revaluation of the Baroque, there is a vast amount of stuff that is merely sweetstuff. It amounts to no more than leaving the gilt on the gingerbread and using chocolate-boxes for ceilings and walls. We must not altogether forget that sweetstuff is a childish taste; and of such is the kingdom of heaven; but I think it is fair to say that some of the children of the Church were allowed to eat too many sweets. Next, in the midst of all this pink sunset of the Renaissance, there appear quite abruptly bright and bracing glimpses of the hard white morning of Christianity. The restoration of the antiquated apse, with its almost Byzantine stiffness and simplicity, looks for an instant like the glimpse into the lost heaven of another and older religion. Its gold is not gilt on any gingerbread, but is of the same substance as the sun. Only it is the remote and quiet sun of a sort of everlasting sunrise. It does exactly express in design and colour what Mr. W. B. Yeats has admirably expressed in metre and words, in his recent poem called "Sailing to Byzantium," about the starkly intellectual appeal of the old Greek Christian art:

> O sages standing in God's holy fire
> As in the gold mosaic of a wall.

And indeed a man might have sailed a long voyage in a ship when he takes the few steps from the gilding of the railings to the gold of the apse. He has come suddenly to a strange country, where stags stand stiffly beside an almost crooked cross and saints are of different sizes, as if all planes of perspective had met. Something in the very distortion belonging to the half dome of an apse lends to such fine archaic design a sort of extra mystery; it almost recalls the shameless mysticism of Professor Einstein, when he says, "All space is slightly curved." This Christian mysticism is felt in an absolute form in the apse; in a relative and realistic form in the fine picture of Giotto

[98]

which hangs in the church, witnessing to the more human, but still childish, vigour and sincerity of the true Middle Ages. When I was young the most advanced art critics would have said that the Byzantine mosaic represented the darkness before the dawn and Giotto the true daybreak of art. Now the most advanced critics will probably say that the archaic apse holds the last glow of art and Giotto is the dusk of its disappearance, which seems to have begun rather early. But I will leave them to fight it out; it is evidently essential to advance critics to be always going further and further back.

But though St. John Lateran contains things good by the ordinary Renaissance rule, and two things very good which are exceptions to the rule, they are not the two things of which I speak. Tourists will certainly be told to stop before the Giotto; and even to look at the apse with some metaphysical blindness to the altar. But there are on each side of the altar two things to which I fancy that foreigners are blinder still; because they are entirely modern. Only I am a little interested in them, being modern myself. I believe that I belong to a Church that is still alive; anyhow I know I belong to a world that is still alive; and those two modern monuments testify to two movements of the modern world. I am not less, but more interested, because the monuments themselves are of recent date. They link themselves with the living Italy in the streets outside; and if anybody does not know that Italy is living, he had better come and see.

The first monument was erected by, and the second monument erected to, the great Pope Leo XIII, the builder of the bridge between modern democracy and the Church. The first monument was at his direction designed and dedicated to that mediæval man who was his hero and whom he made in some sense his model; the famous Innocent III who played so determining a part in the central problems of the Middle Ages; the Crusades and the Franciscan movement. The sculptured tomb is very good of its kind, like many of these neglected modern works in Rome. But it is not for that sort of merit that I pause beside it or ask the reader to consider it. The whole form and character of it, as compared with this Renaissance church where it stands, is a singularly compact and complete statement of something rather rare in Rome, though common in Romanism and in the whole Romanized world. It is the modern resurrection of Mediævalism. It is as important in history as the Renaissance resurrection of Paganism. I will say something in a moment of its social and spiritual meaning, of which its critics are curiously and almost comically ignorant. But the immediate point is that the modern Pope has not only entombed the mediæval Pope, but has gone as far as possible towards giving him a mediæval tomb. Within the square framework, with its black marble picked out with stars, necessitated by the scheme of the whole building, is a sort of secret grotto of the Gothic and a sepulchre that might have been made for Hugh of Lin-

coln or Thomas of Canterbury by his own followers and
friends. Here, lying flat in the patient and pious posture of
a humbler age, is the Pope who first blessed the Poor
Brothers and sat in judgment on the Kings. Here a great
modern mind, one of the greatest of modern minds, has
deliberately made a modern tomb as a mediæval tomb.
That, if we consider it, is a notable and significant sequel
to that long series of Papal tombs to be found in St.
Peter's; the Popes of the sixteenth, the seventeenth and
the eighteenth centuries; rioting, one may say, in every
technical trick and dancing balance of the Baroque,
using to the full all that modern science and ingenuity
can teach of tilted poise or muscular equilibrium; in these
artistic matters at least turning their backs for ever on the
past. With this monument we have the last great modern
return to the past. This, among the last of such sculptured
figures, has literally lain down with his fathers; with his
remote fathers of the days of Dominic and the Poverello.
On his right is an armed figure emblematic of the Crusades, on his left a figure of Wisdom as she cried aloud
in the streets of mediæval Paris and Oxford.

In this rough study, which is devoted to resurrections,
it is well to pause and remember how much the whole
modern movement has been a return of the mediæval
movement. The thing has been repeated too often to be
a coincidence or a romantic mistake. One generation, if
seeking no more than picturesqueness and adventure
amid the rising rigidity of Utilitarianism, found it in

mediæval romance, if chiefly in mediæval ruins; in Melrose by moonlight or Torquilstone in flames. Another generation, seeking only earnest Churchmanship in a Protestant Church, found its models in the Saxon Saints and Gothic monkeries of the Oxford Movement. Yet again a generation, generally speaking the next generation, seeking some decorative scheme to dignify and beautify the brutal ugliness of manufacturing England, found it in the illuminated texts and coloured chronicles of William Morris studying Geoffrey Chaucer. And now yet a fourth generation, seeking for some social principle, in economics and politics, that shall be a human alternative to the individualistic muddle of Manchester and the insane centralization of Moscow, has found it at least generally indicated in the nature, and even proclaimed in the name, of the great guilds of the Middle Ages. These things are not coincidences; seldom has one whole period like the present fed so repeatedly and persistently on one whole period of the past.

The modern world has already been mediævalized. It is too late for our simple friends to cry out against going back to mediæval things. For nearly a hundred years we have done nothing else. Because even Scott among Scottish Puritans could see that Melrose was beautiful, therefore even to-day the Baptist Chapel is built in bad Gothic and no longer in bad classical architecture. It is too late to hide the fact that there is still such a thing as Exeter Cathedral and no longer such a thing as Exeter Hall.

Because even Oxford dons could see that Saxon Saints were in earnest, as eighteenth-century bishops were not in earnest, nobody now proposes to wear a black eighteenth-century gown instead of a surplice. Because people in peg-top trousers sitting on horsehair sofas were hideous and knew that they were hideous, they could not resist the new scheme of natural decorative dress and furniture which William Morris had learned from the study of old missals and mediæval tapestries. And because mediæval society was at least a society, with social institutions, even an atheist cannot be such a fool as to talk any longer about enlightened self-interest or the individual standing alone. I might even agree that, in a sense, the modern world has been mediævalized enough. But those who say it cannot be mediævalized died some decades before they began to say so.

There was not room in the small and crowded city of Rome for another Renaissance. There would indeed have been something like an earthquake, if the modern mediævalists had tried to rebuild the Rome of Innocent, where so many Popes had tried to rebuild the Rome of Augustus. The traveller strolling through the town will see few nooks and corners in which to place the Cathedral of Beauvais or the great tower of Salisbury. But intellectually something like such a renaissance did take place and is exactly represented by the Pontificate of Leo XIII. The Papal support of the Trade Union movement, with its clearly defined principles for association within the

State, owed almost everything to the study and under-standing of the great mediæval associations. It would be easy to mention a score of matters in which the Catholic justification of the Trade Union was based on the justice of the Guild. But of all that mediæval movement in the modern world nothing plastic and tangible remains in Rome except this one recumbent figure and almost Gothic canopy in the monument of Innocent III. For the most part the pure lovers of the Gothic wander through Rome not only hungry but starved. It seems to me all the more worthy of note, therefore, that the Pope of the modern popular movement planned, not without severity, the one mediæval tomb.

It is all the more remarkable, I might say amusing, because he was not allowed to play any such mediæval tricks with his own tomb. The monument of Leo XIII himself, which stands on the other side to balance that which he built for his predecessor, represents what I can only call a riotous relapse into the Baroque. Leo XIII is not even represented as ritually blessing the faithful with the almost menacing vigour of the figures in St. Peter's. He is merely waving his hand to them with almost hila-rious benevolence; as if he were saying, "So long!" or "Ta-Ta!" rather than "Benedicat." There could hardly be a quainter contrast than that between the modest but manly figure that he made of Innocent and the rollicking rococo figure that other people made of him. Which may be used by some as an argument to show that the spirit of the Baroque has taken final possession of Rome and is not to be expelled, but breaks out again at the first opportunity in spite of precept or example; dancing even on the grave of a mediævalist the moment he is dead. Only there happens to be something else on the monument besides the buoyant and almost breezy figure of the benevolent Pontiff. On one side is a figure of Christendom bowed down like a widow and holding only the plain primitive cross of timber that covers the widest delimitation of Christianity. And on the other is a labourer leaning on the tools of his trade, and lifting a hand in salutation of him who wrote, across the open optimistic pages of modern economists of the manufacturing age, the words not to be forgotten; that the rich of our time have laid upon the toiling masses of mankind a yoke little better than slavery.

I have deliberately dwelt upon these two entirely modern sculptures (competent and effective like nearly all these Italian sculptures, but not of any special importance or originality in the world of art) because they illustrate the moral which I most strongly desire to draw. That unless a man understands that Rome is a modern city, he does not understand that it is an eternal city. Refusing to look at its modern monuments is but a way of saying it is a dead city. Yet any one who visits it with the notion that it is a dead city will find it a city most monstrously miraculous; a city in which the dead can walk. The truth is that nobody who will not follow its recent and real development will be able to make head or tail of it; not even, as I have said, if he seeks its head in the Capitol and its tail in the stop-press news. To understand it we must not be content with the present or the remote past. We must remember what most men instantly forget; the recent past. We must understand the whole meaning of a period like that covered by the Pontificate of Pope Leo XIII. For that reason, and merely as a part of the argument, I have paused before his monument; but I admit it is with other and deeper and quite indescribable emotions that I have paused before his grave.

The Reformation is always described as a protest against the power of the Pope. I should rather describe it as a protest against the impotence of the Pope. It did not come in a time like that of Innocent III, when the Pope was really powerful. It came at the end of a long trail of tragi-comedy and bathos, in which the central power, so far from being too central, had been hopelessly decentralized and divided. It was not until people had had the absurd experience of having three Popes that they completed the absurdity by having three or four religions. In short, from the high moment of the Middle Ages, about the time of Innocent III, there was a long decline of mediæval strength and unity; which went step by step with the decline in the dignity of the Pope. From the first, of course, there had been some disadvantages in the Papal position, even at its best; there

Kings and all the powers of the earth have striven in vain to break the thrice glorious chains of Peter, which bind him to his palace even as they did to his prison.

And then, like a thunderclap, came the strangest ending of the strange story that began long before when the Pope turned his back on Byzantium. As we have noted, he not only turned his back on civilization, when he turned his back on Byzantium; he also turned his face to barbarism. He made a treaty with the tribes of the wild North and West and eventually erected among them a new half-barbarian empire, to balance in some small degree the overpowering prestige of the New Rome in the East and the great Patriarchs of the great Greek cities, ruling the rich and cultured lands under the crown of Constantine. The wild Western experiment in the person of Charlemagne had been an empire almost as brief as a revolution. There seemed, on the other hand, no reason why the calm and stately court of Constantinople should not go on for ages like the Empire of China. Only, as already hinted, something had happened; something that can always happen and can never be expected. A man named Mahomet had lived and died and become a destiny and a driving storm in the souls of men, that began to pour across the great Greek world like a deluge. The rich lands and ities were submerged; the great golden Patriarchs w chased out like beggars; the whole of that civilization hat had sought to overpower the Papacy, in the war the images, was itself overpowered;

and (by a queer irony) overpowered by more simple and violent image-breakers. The Iconoclasts of the desert slew the Iconoclasts of the city. At last, after a long agony of heroic resistance, the city itself fell. The last of the Greek Cæsars died sword in hand; and since that day the New Rome, the name that was a spell on the whole world, has been a rather dirty town of the Turks.

Such was the end of the first and seemingly the most successful attempt to move Rome from Rome. Naturally it left the Pope, restored to his own see, in an entirely new position towards the Patriarchs his rivals; who were now Bishops without sees. It has also been said that the crash scattered the Byzantine scholars and artists and so stimulated the Renaissance; and there is something in it, but less than is often supposed. The real roots of Renaissance Rome were Roman.

Meanwhile the interregnum had ended in what seemed like a reign of Antichrist; because it was the reign of Anti-Popes. A Pope could be established in Rome, but another claimant could continue his Papacy at Avignon; and at one time there was even a third claimant somewhere else. This intensified the nationalist split in Europe, one nation following one Pope and one another; and the confusion of ecclesiastical authority, among other shameful accidents, cast a momentary but mortal shadow upon the shining figure of Joan of Arc. But it had another effect less easy to describe. The Papacy shrank; men began to regard the Pope with a new feeling that he was a local prince instead of a universal priest. The scandal of rivalry was stopped; but the Councils which stopped it tended rather to restrict the Papacy. The Pope who returned to Rome returned to the Roman City but never again to the Roman Empire. He had hardly returned before the last agony of Christendom began; and all that preceded the vague and yet violent restlessness of Luther. At the time the far more pressing peril of Christendom appeared in the last onslaughts of Islam; the new Moslem invasion which stretches broadly from the great disaster of Mohacs to the great rescue of Lepanto. The Reformation has been called many things, good and bad; and there was certainly much in it both defensible and indefensible. But that is the thing about it which I for one find it hardest to forgive. It was a Christian mutiny during a Moslem invasion.

As the Popes narrowed as pontiffs they did in a sense broaden as princes; they did at least strengthen as princes. Their kingdom was smaller and yet it was more imperialistic; if you will, their kingdom was more of this world. But at least it was as wide as this world; in the sense of stretching out to the arts and sciences of this world. The fighting Popes who led armies and set up the castles of the Campagna, were often men who opened their gates to the greatest artists of history and their minds to the profoundest problems of philosophy. Their wickedness has been considerably exaggerated; there was only one of them who was very wicked, and he was

mostly wicked because his favourite son was wickeder.
Alexander Borgia may indeed be regarded as a highly
pious and orthodox argument for the celibacy of the
clergy. But it is true that the Popes were political and in
the wrong sense local. It was about this time that most
people became suddenly and vividly conscious that the
Pope was an Italian. A large number of previous Popes
had of course been Italian, though many had been of
other nations, Spanish, French or English; but men had
thought of them as European. Or if they thought of them
otherwise, it was not as Italian but as Roman; and that
because it was more universal to be Roman than to be
European. But Rome was now a principality, and rather
a small and struggling and jealous principality; its religious scope had been rather diminished by Basle and
Constance long before Worms and Spires. Thus, viewed
in one aspect, and possibly the highest aspect, we
may say that the Roman bishopric at the end of the
Middle Ages was at the lowest ebb of discredit and
dubious transformation. It had suffered endless humilia-
tions; had been trailed in the mire across Europe, had
been put up to auction by upstarts bidding against each
other, and was close to the final crash when whole nations
should be lost in the night. And yet in that last and dark-
est hour, it did after all do something. It made Rome; it
built the mighty city that we see; it filled the sky with
the dome of St. Peter's and heaved against the clouds the
limbs of the last giants of Michael Angelo; it showed, at

the last and worst, how gigantic are the things that can
be done in a little space. But above all it effected another
and a new sort of resurrection, which will be noted in the
next chapter.

But though this marks the emergence from the Middle
Ages, which in Rome remain only as one of its long but
dark and buried tunnels, I am still dreaming of the
dream of Innocent III; and of that other whose absence
haunts me like a presence. It was but a moment, as it
were, that he lingered under the pillars of that portico,
speaking to the Pope, who mistook him for some ragged
herd from the hills; he went back swiftly to his own
Umbrian uplands, with his own light and impulsive
movement, and there amid the shrines of Assisi he still
stands in a native and mediæval air. They lately erected
a fine statue of him in front of the church in Rome;
but in the interval the associations of his name have
hardly been specially Roman. But I cannot forget the
deeper reality of the dream; and I see him as Innocent
saw him, not so much in front of the church as under
it; one of the pillars propping a falling house. I can almost fancy that he is now literally under it, buried with
so much of the Middle Ages in the very vaults of Rome;
the greatest and most glorious of mediæval men sustaining like a column the whole work of the after ages and
the later arts which have in some sense crushed or buried
him; St. Francis still upholding the Church as Atlas upheld the world. He at least would be a very Gothic

pillar to uphold all that Classic and Baroque architecture; with his hairy rags as of a goatherd and eager pointed beard and face fanatical with forgiveness. Stevenson speaks of unfrowning caryatids bearing the falling heavens; and no caryatid so unfrowning as Francis could be found to bear those seven heavens of ever sinking stone. The vision of Innocent was true in more ways than one. The personality he met for a moment not only saved Catholicism at a moment when it might have gone down before Islam and a hundred heresies; but he has been in history the support of all the building and painting and carving that came after him; and has truly established the Church, even the modern Church of St. John Lateran. That is why it is necessary to sketch here, however rudely, the interlude of Roman mediævalism, so important in history, so invisible in Rome. And therefore St. Francis still stands as a statue that is also a column; the living pillar of the Lateran.

IV · THE RETURN OF THE GODS

The name of Resurrectionist had a horrible meaning, at once grotesque and grisly, as applied to those who dug up dead men in the interests of science. It might seem somewhat harsh to use it of those who dug up dead gods in the interests of art. Nevertheless, Resurrectionism is a word that is wanted in a wider sense. Nor indeed would it be entirely fanciful to compare the Renaissance of Rome in the early sixteenth century with the Resurrectionism in Edinburgh in the early nineteenth. When the stern and scientific Scot gazes with Puritan severity at the palaces of the Borgias, it might be pleasant to prod him with a light-hearted allusion to the later legend of the Body-Snatchers. It is unfair to say that a surgical operation is needed to introduce a joke to a Scotsman; but anyhow some very grim jokes were needed to introduce him to a surgical operation. And if he says that this art of antiquity was indebted to the patronage of mere lust and luxury, it might be suggested that the science of anatomy was indebted at the start to a systematic campaign of murder. If there was in the sixteenth-century festivity a certain element of a dance of death, it would seem that the northern doctors did not disapprove of death but only of dancing. At the end of the mediæval epoch it was apparently possible, and indeed usual, for the same people to combine scientific curiosity and artistic beauty; in the modern epoch those who started the scientific curiosity started it in conditions of almost bestial ugliness. And though the comparison is here but a parenthesis it is something of a parable; and in nothing more than this; that, with whatever defensible objects, the body-snatchers dug up complete bodies in order to dismember and scatter them, while the antiquaries of the Renaissance dug up scattered limbs and features of stone in order to fit them together into the statues that still amaze the world. It is a hackneyed business to talk of analysis and synthesis; but considering only the complete conception of the body, it is true to say that Leonardo could take it to pieces but also put it together again. That combination of curiosity with creation has not been revived in the modern world. That is a Resurrectionism that has not been resurrected.

But there is another and stranger sense of analogy suggested by those early Italian archæologists gathering up from field and river-bed the broken gods of their remote fathers. They might in a more serious sense be called Resurrection men; since it was exactly so that their religious pictures and parables conceived the Last Trumpet as gathering from all the ends of the earth the scattered bodies and even the separated bones of mankind. It had terrible aspects, more easily conceived in turbulent times, but it was at least a summons to life and not to death, to completeness and not to corruption or dissolution; to the remarriage of mind and body and not to the infinite subdivision of body and disappearance of mind. Above all, this old creative curiosity had a savour of Resurrection, because its spontaneity and swiftness swept over the world almost in the manner of a miracle. It happened so quickly, as historical movements go, that it did seem as if the last dry bones of the Middle Ages clothed themselves with flesh at the sound of a trumpet. It did seem as if God Himself had commanded the dead gods to be gathered and to arise and stand; and it is something in that spirit or suggestion that makes all purely pagan treatment of the Renaissance fail and ring false to us, when we actually stand before its monuments. About the Renaissance there was something mystical, since its origin was after all mediæval; and there went along with all its curiosity a confidence which a modern would call credulity.

Christianity is the religion of the Resurrection; in which it differs, for instance, from Buddhism, which is the religion of the Recurrence or Return, which in practice means little more than what men of science used to call the Conservation of Energy. That is, the idea that every elemental force or expression returns in some form; but the form does not return. When Mr. H. G. Wells said that Buddhism was fully in accordance with our modern ideas, this is what he meant. It resembles our modern ideas in many respects, including that of being no longer modern. The Conservation of Energy seemed the most obvious of cosmic principles; and modern philosophers have a taste in the obvious. It is supremely typical of our time that when a score of modern philosophers had founded their modern philosophies on this solid fact of science, the men of science began to discover that it is not a fact. But however that quarrel between modern rationalism and more modern science may stand at the moment, it is broadly true that any number of philosophies, ancient and modern, have assumed this cosmic conservation and recurrence, from the large philosophy of Buddha to the much more limited philosophy of Herbert Spencer. Sometimes this philosophy accepts some form of Immortality. But it is always in the form of Reincarnation and not Resurrection. More often it adopts one of St. Thomas Aquinas's arguments against Immortality (which that almost irritatingly fair-minded rationalist carefully ranges against himself) and argues that a thing will never recover its identity when once it has really lost its form. Nothing but the Christian Creed has ever had the audacity to assert that a thing will actually recover its identity because it will recover its form. That is what the Anglican Bishop of Birmingham means by calling the Christian religion materialistic. And that is why a material argument was offered to another St. Thomas, who was also something of a rationalist.

The history of Christianity cannot be understood unless it is realized that it started with the staggering miracle of a dead man who was a live man, and who was not a ghost. It was not merely the spirit triumphing over the body; it was the body triumphing over the tomb. There are any number of admirable people who cannot believe in this story. But for the argument here, we do not ask them for belief in it; we only ask them for belief in the belief in it. We ask them to consider an interesting historical idea and development; and not to be too irritated to understand it merely because they do not believe in it. For it is the key to very nearly everything in the development of two thousand years; and in nothing is it so much the key to Christendom as in the recurrent reversions to Paganism.

Every educated person has heard over and over again the phrase "The Renaissance." Nearly every educated person (and many much more valuable but imperfectly educated persons) have read a text in their Bibles which runs, "Unless a man be born again." Few among the educated or uneducated persons have ever stopped to notice that the two phrases are exactly the same phrase, translated into French or English. And though there is a great deal more to be said, both good and bad, about what we call the Renaissance of the sixteenth century in Europe, the first fact to be seized about it is that it was emphatically a Christian movement; because it was a Renaissance; because it was a Resurrection. Nobody but a Christian was ever mad enough to dig up anything so dead as that. We all understand the sense in which it is called Pagan, for it was certainly in that sense a resurrection of Paganism. But only the Paganism was Pagan; not the resurrection. I think it highly doubtful whether any real Pagans would ever have attempted anything so romantic and ridiculous. The ancient Greeks did not attempt to reconstruct the whole daily life of the ancient Egyptians. The notion that when the mansions of Marius and Camillus had mouldered into dust of one thousand five hundred years, when their gods were forbidden and forgotten, when every detail of their daily ritual was lost, when a new universal religion from the East had exterminated their old religion and in its turn grown old, that anything could persuade a whole generation of human beings to live again that lost antiquity like a masquerade—that would have seemed to almost any heathen a mere insult to his heathen common sense. That the reading of a few manuscripts should madden men who had never heard of Martial or Catullus before, to imitate those men in the carving of their door-posts or the exact metre of their love-songs, was the manifestation of a new sort of human vitality. There ran through the whole of it a rage of material reconstruction. It was no question of a moral maxim, of wise and wide application, handed down from some primitive philosopher; of some universal commandment carved in stone or proclaimed by a prehistoric prophet; of the remote founder of a religion bequeathing some idea that could still be used as an idea. It was a question of carving, building, painting, dressing and as far as possible talking like men who had been dead for fifteen centuries. There was a lust for detail, especially domestic detail. There was that almost arrogant obtrusion, there was that almost wearisome repetition, which even to this day lends something overpowering and crushing to the works of the classical Renaissance. The mediæval idea of making an image was almost lost in the crowds of gesticulating statues. The mediæval idea of going to a shrine was almost forgotten in cities of jostling and competing temples. In a sense it was Paganism. In a sense it was almost Polytheism. But there was written across all that solid exuberance the strangest of mortal words: The Resurrection of the Body.

The more sensitive complain of the Renaissance sculptors that they made Christ as solid and material as Venus. It is a more just complaint that they made Venus as solid as Christ. The corporeal reality belongs to Christ rising from the tomb and not Venus rising from the sea. But if we would understand the real relations of the Church to the Pagans we must go back to things more grim and rigid and more archaic. Let us begin with an obelisk; no Puritan, however sensitive, will find the allurements of Venus in an obelisk; nor has any lover of Cleopatra been caught embracing Cleopatra's Needle. I will therefore take the most obvious example. The obelisk of the Piazza del Popolo is in itself very ancient and unique, having been raised in adoration of the Egyptian Sun-God, Ra, in the time of Rameses the Third, famous as the Pharaoh who consented to the exodus of Moses and the Israelites. Being taken to Rome, it was rededicated to Apollo, the Sun-God of the Latins, if I remember right, by the Emperor Augustus. Now this also stands surmounted by a cross and in front of a Christian Church, the Church of Santa Maria del Popolo; and bearing a Latin inscription pertinent and to our purpose. I find this inscription somewhat quaintly translated, in an excellent little guide-book written for Englishmen, but I should imagine by Italians; and Italians unaware of some nuances of our national speech. "Before the sanctuary of the one, in whose womb the Sun of Justice was born, under the reign of Augustus, I arise more cheerful and with more dignity."

There is something pleasing in the thought of a hoary and primeval Egyptian monolith announcing that it rises more cheerful and with more dignity. It is as if it were all the better for a sea voyage, and had been quite bright at breakfast on the following day. But the announcement, however we translate it, is profoundly true. And it is the truth most necessary to grasp if we are to begin to understand the part played by Rome in history. It is not only a joke about being bright at breakfast; it is a very serious fact that this stone, once dedicated to two sun-gods, now stands in a light that is brighter than twenty suns. If the jest in any way obscures it, I will try my hand here at rendering what I imagine it to mean, in parallel English phrases; it would have to read something like this: "Before her shrine of whose body was born the very Sun of Justice, in the Empire of Augustus, more joyfully and with a nobler dignity I arise."

What is to be done with the dingy and inky little people who laboriously prove to us that Christianity (if they are atheists) or Catholicism (if they are Protestants) is "only" a rehash of Paganism or borrowed its ideas from the Pagans? A man standing here in Rome is reduced to silence; he can only answer that such stupidity is stupefying. It is rather as if somebody said that Science may pretend to be independent, but it has really stolen all its facts from Nature; or that Protestants professed to be Christians, and yet filched things from the sacred books of the Jews. Science boasts of being based on Nature; and Protestants, when they were Protestants, boasted of being based on the Bible. Christian Rome boasts of being built on Pagan Rome; or surmounting and transcending, but also of preserving it. From the thousand carven throats of the city, from the hollow wreathing horns of the Tritons, from the golden mouths of the trumpets, from the jaws of flamboyant lions and the lips of rhetorical attitudinizing statues, from everything that can be imagined to speak or testify, there is as it were one solid silent roar of exultation and

victory: "We have saved Old Rome; we have resurrected Old Rome; we have resurrected Pagan Rome,
save that it is more Roman for not being Pagan." There
is no question of hiding the connection between the two
epochs; the new epoch emphasizes every point at which it
touches the old. Nearly every Christian Church is carefully built on the site of a Pagan temple. In one place it
distinguishes a particular church by combining the name
of Maria with that of Minerva. In another place it pre-
serves the seven niches of the Pagan Planets for seven
corresponding Christian Saints. Up on the rock of the Ara
Cœli the little broken altar of the temple of Augustus is
carefully preserved, like a relic, inside the larger Christian building; that men may remember how even a
heathen looked in that place for an altar of heaven. There
is no question of the Church disguising Pagan ideas as
Christian ideas, for there never was any disguise about
the matter. The heathen things the Church preserved she
preserved openly. The heathen things she destroyed she
destroyed openly. If on the whole she destroyed first and
preserved afterwards there was a frank and national reason, as we shall see. And she preserved some things and
destroyed others for a reason which these dismal rationalists cannot use their reason enough to understand.
Science finds its facts in Nature, but Science is not Nature; because Science has co-ordinated ideas, interpreta-
tions and analyses; and can say of Nature what Nature
cannot say for itself. The Faith finds its facts and prob-

lems in humanity, even heathen humanity; but the Faith is not merely humanity; because it brings to it principles of life and order and understanding, and comprehends humanity as humanity cannot comprehend itself. And it is not true, but totally false, to say that these principles, in the sense in which they are valued by Catholics, were equally known to Pagans. If you had said to any Pagan in the street, "Jupiter died for love of you as though there were no other man alive and every time you sin, you torture him anew," the Pagan would not have had the wildest notion of what you were talking about.

The essential word is written on the obelisk; the Sun of Justice. The sun the heathen worshipped had not been a sun of justice; and had not pretended to be. It was a sun of beauty, a sun of terror, and sometimes most gloriously a sun of joy; but not of justice. Nobody understands Paganism who does not realize that its highest gods could be irresponsible like goblins and elves; friendly but also capricious or cruel. It may be said that some things attributed to the Christian God were unjust; but that is not the point. They were not conceived as unjust; they were, at worst, excesses of a fury for justice. But nobody who told the story of Niobe or Marsyas told it to show that the Sun-God was just. He was constantly doing things that had no more to do with justice than a pestilence. On the balance, it is strictly true that the Christians got the sunshine and the Pagans got the sunstroke. In short, the Christians had a theory of cosmic justice, right or wrong, controlling the mere caprice which did not even pretend to be just; and in having that the followers of the Sun of Justice did think they had eclipsed the Sun of the Sun-Worshippers. But so far from wishing to conceal the great works of the Sun-Worshippers, they went out of their way to display them. So far from hiding the fact that they inherited much from their heathen fathers, they filled Rome with proclamations which positively brag of their inheritance. To any one looking at such an obelisk, the truth is obvious. Paganism is left in full view, all the bird-headed gods and sacred serpents graven on the stone; and a cross merely clapped on the top, almost like a sort of iron hat; as much as to say, "That will keep you quiet." The heathen splendours are shown, but perhaps it is rather as the captive kings were shown in a triumph. Doubtless, some heathen things were not shown; and a good thing too. Doubtless, in a case like the cross on the obelisk, there was some vague sense among sensitive Christians that signing it with the cross was safer; for fear it should walk. But anyhow, there is no disguise of the Pagan part or the additional and even artificial character of the Christian part. Nothing could be more unlike people secretly indebted to mythology and ashamed of their debt.

The desire of all nations, the dream of all religions, the imaginative craving that in some way something heroic might save the sufferings that are human—that indeed existed everywhere and that was the need which the

Gospel was sent to supply. But the need was not the same as the supply. And the supply was a supply of perfectly definite and even detailed moral and metaphysical ideas which nobody but a fool could possibly identify with myths. And the sceptic only makes a fool of himself, when he first complains that Catholic dogmas are dogmatic, that they are in their nature precise claims to a knowledge of unknowable things; and then pretends that he can find these very precise dogmas in the irresponsible and inconsistent fairyland of heathen mythology. If the Catholic doctrine of Christ is a hard, positive, inflexible, infallible dogma imposed on the intellect, then it most certainly is not like the Greek story of Hercules. Some may think theology a bad thing; but those who believe in it naturally think it a good thing, and they are at least quite certain that the Pagans were never theologians. There never was a theology about Jupiter and Juno and Hercules. But if there was not a theology still less was there a theodicy, or any systematic attempt to justify the ways of gods to men.

That is the deep significance of the inscription about the Sun of Justice. That is the meaning of the "cheerful" or confident tone of the obelisk. The men who so inscribed it had not the smallest doubt, nor have I, that they knew a great deal more about the Sun than the Sun-Worshipper. To hear some of the critics talk, one would think that the Christians had secretly stolen the sun out of the sky, and, having pinched it from paganism, attempted to hide it from posterity. The Christians knew quite well that the sun was a grand golden object and that people had worshipped it; they were not afraid of it, they were not ashamed of using it as an instrument or symbol of worship; only it was the worship of something better. They thought the Catholic philosophy about the Sun of Justice was something entirely superior to a Solar Myth; and so it was. They were not in the least disposed to hide the matters in which the inferior thing had suggested the superior; though they were ready, sometimes to excess, to denounce the errors of the inferior when it contradicted the superior. It was about the superiority that they had no doubt: Santa Maria sopra Minerva.

The muddle has arisen because men started again to study mythology when they had abruptly refused to study theology; chiefly because it was Calvinist theology. They rather hurriedly advanced the view that we can have no knowledge of theistic things. When they were very muddle-headed they maintained that we can have theism without theology. But there is a perfectly fair case for those who threw over the whole problem as insoluble; those who adopted what is commonly called Agnosticism. But even men who know nothing cannot settle everything. And even men who follow their reason as far as it will go, cannot contradict themselves without limit, or have it both ways every time. And if they refuse to read any theology, they cannot say that everything in it is to be found in mythology. And, as a mere matter of fact, it is not. Ideas like the true doctrines of Fruition, of Free Will, of the Hypostatic Union of the Immaculate Conception, of Expiation and Purgatory, are in every possible sense ideas; positive ideas; to the ordinary human mind additional ideas; in the only permanent sense new ideas. It is all nonsense to say that they can be found in the ritual of Adonis or the cult of Atys; they can not. The answer of the Agnostic to these mystical ideas is that he does not know anything about them; not that ancient Ionians or Egyptians knew all about them. They knew nothing of the sort, and they would have been the first to say so. The ancients were Agnostics, as the moderns are Agnostics. Between them stands something different from anything else. It may be mad; but it is certainly different.

The distinction must be made very distinct, because it is exactly that which throws into sharp relief the extraordinary experiment of the Renaissance. Whatever else it was, it most emphatically was not the action of men who had merely veiled the Venus as the Virgin and now raised the veil; or who had set on the head of Jupiter a stone mask of Christ and now could throw off the mask. Anybody who knows the deep and even painful intensity of the most ascetic mediæval art will know better than that. It was a deliberate revival of the forms of the old mythology; but because the forms were now lifeless, not because the gods were still alive. It would be truer to say that the world had waited until it was safe to see once more the faces of the forsaken gods. If they dug up a dead religion, they dug it up because it was dead. None of them, as I shall remark, had the least doubt that his own religion was alive. Nevertheless, though we may say in this sense that they had waited till it was safe, it was not yet by any means self-evident to everybody that it was safe. Indeed, if we may judge by the modern misunderstanding in the North and the shrill cry of the Puritans against the Pagans who painted the palaces of the Pope, it was not safe. The authorities of the Catholic Church really took a considerable risk when they threw themselves with such reckless generosity, from the very beginning, into the revival of Greek and Italian art. That Pope of the Dark Ages who defied the golden palace of Byzantium in defence of the right to make statues, was certainly supported with equal courage by the Popes of the Renaissance when there were some more defiant and sometimes perhaps less defensible statues to be made. But the Pope is always pelted as much for defending the rights of the world as the rights of the Church.

It is believed, somewhat inaccurately, that there is a conviction among Catholics that the Pope cannot possibly be wrong. Anyhow, there is a more solidly supported conviction among Anti-Catholics that the Pope cannot possibly be right, which seems an even more special and supernatural distinction. There would seem to rest upon him alone a mysterious cloud, not of inerrancy but of inevitable errancy. This may seem fanciful to the fastidious; but it is very common among many people who boast of their common sense. The people in the Protestant countries, who for generations flatly refused to use the new astronomical calendar, merely because it was offered to them by the Pope, would certainly have based their action on their sturdy common sense. The newspapers might occasionally by the way mention that incident, as well as the incident of Galileo, since they are so passionately preoccupied with the progress of astronomy. But in sober truth it is no exaggeration to say that in many such sturdy political constitutions, as the King can do no wrong, so the Pope can do no right. I have already dwelt a little on one historical incident, because it related to some outstanding features of Rome; the example of the Papal decision on the lawfulness of statues. I defy anybody of sense to say that, on a point like that, the No Popery critics would not have had it both ways, or either way. If the Pontiff had condemned images, would they not say it was a Papal veto on sculpture? If he allowed images, will they not say it was a Papal permit for idolatry? And this sort of dilemma recurs with almost every discussion; and specially concerns the discussion about the luxury and laxity of the Renaissance. Nobody says there was nothing to be condemned in any parts of the Papal action. But everybody must admit that anything would have been condemned; and that if their action had been the exact opposite, it would have been condemned more.

To put the matter shortly; they would have been abused if they had been merely mediæval. They are abused because they were not merely mediæval. And then they are called mediæval after all, merely because mediæval is a term of abuse. Nobody need have been very much surprised if they had been merely mediæval, in the sense of clinging close to the special and splendid but sometimes limited things of the Middle Ages; to the Gothic in architecture, to the Scholastic in philosophy; to the pointed arch and the pointed argument. It would have been no very inexcusable narrowness, if they really had been contented to be as broad as St. Thomas Aquinas or as deep as Dante or as high as the spire of Old St. Paul's. Mediævalism had its vices, which idiots imagine us to deny, but it had a system that had seen Europe survive like one nation through shock after shock of barbarian war and oriental pestilence; and no great shame would lie upon prudent rulers and guardians of the past, if they had preserved all the details and disciplines of the past, rather than trust themselves to a new and perhaps anarchic future. But, as a fact, the Popes did trust to the future. They trusted with very unusual hope and confidence to the future. It was not their mistake alone, if trusting to the future is sometimes only trusting to the fashion. Anyhow, they were in the forefront of the fashion; and were the leaders of the age towards its own particular vision of liberty and light. But the very men who would have mocked at them for clinging to the Middle Ages still sternly reprove them for accepting the Renaissance. If a Pope read Plato he was called a hedonist and a heathen, and if he had only read Aristotle, he would have been called a fanatical old fool. If a Pope dug up Greek marbles, he was worshipping strange gods; if he was satisfied with grey Gothic stones, he was a survival from the twilight of the Goths. We are familiar with those two horns of the dilemma, which look a little like the two horns of the devil. At least that shape and shadow has always been thrown upon the wall in the presence of that light. "We have piped to you and you have not danced; we have mourned to you and you have not lamented."

The Popes have paid heavily for their support of progress, and their belief in education and the advancement of learning. If they had always been behind the times, they would by this time be quite in the fashion. They have for a moment lost their chance among the Modernists through having so often been Modern. Because there are too many competent convincing classical statues in St. John Lateran, because there is too much workmanlike Renaissance sculpture in Rome, because they multiplied gods and heroes till men grew weary of them as of a common crowd, because they cheapened and popularized anatomy and physiology and perspective, till many men could do the trick and most men could

[135]

apply the test—because they thus gorged and glutted the world with good work of the sort that the whole world then desired, they have suffered for their æsthetic generosity and left the world demanding more æsthetic economy. If the statues in St. John Lateran had been stricter and narrower and more monastic, they would have been almost worshipped by Ruskin and Rossetti and the Romantics of the nineteenth century. If they had been blank-faced, harsh-featured, with eyes flat like fishes and drapery as severe as conic sections, they would now be revered, and doubtless rightly revered, by the newer school of Mr. Eric Gill. If they had looked like the lumps of stone that are the idols of the Fiji Islanders, they might have seemed as subtle and sophisticated as the work of Mr. Epstein. I say this without animosity; I have a very great admiration for Mr. Eric Gill, I have no particular quarrel with Mr. Epstein. But it is true to say that the art of Rome would have been nearer to the new spirit of these new masters, if it had never progressed at all. The Popes had only to neglect art; and it would have produced all the naked monsters needed to inspire even the newest of the moderns. But the Popes encouraged art; as they encouraged science and education and most other things. It is a very dangerous thing to do.

At least, that long line of statues in St. John Lateran ought to teach us something about the psychology of this perpetual quarrel of old and new art. What is the matter with them is that there seem to be too many of them, and that they manage to remind us of having seen the same thing too often before. When art has reached that point, it does become natural and even necessary to do something different. But let us remember that what we are asking for is difference rather than dominance. I am puzzled that critics allow so little in this matter for the personal fact of fatigue. If I am compelled to walk ten miles down a stone corridor, engraved on each side with fine reproductions of the Elgin Marbles, it is probable that I shall be rather less thrilled by the last Centaur than I was by the first. But that is no reflection on that particular Centaur, or his status in Centaur society. That does not make any difference to the quality of the carving as it strikes another gentleman just starting cheerfully from the other end. Doubtless I shall emerge from the classic corridor crying out for Gothic gargoyles and Chinese dragons; ready to fall in love with Mr. Epstein's Night or kiss the spacious hands of Rima herself. But my feelings do not affect the works of Phidias or the feelings of more fortunate people about them. It is the custom to say that we must have reform or improvement, but that there is no good in mere change. I am rather inclined to say that we must have change, so long as it does not pretend to be improvement.

Anyhow, that is what is wrong with Rome of the Renaissance. In the vulgar phrase, it is Too Much of a Good Thing. But that ought not to force us to forget that

the thing is good. The achievement of man, by which
he can carve living features and well-balanced bodies,
and imitate the rush or ripple of drapery and muscle, is
a good thing; it is a gift of God; a monkey cannot do it;
a man cannot do it till he has reached a high mastery and
cultural conquest found only on the heights of history.
If we found one of these florid statues for the first time
in a featureless desert, we should know well enough that
it was a wonderful thing. If the art of the future were
really to stretch before us as a corridor decorated only
with broken curves and triangles, if we could advance
not for ten miles but for two or three centuries through
a world of which the whole art was in diagram and dehumanized pattern, if we saw nothing on every side but
the blank planes and proportions of pure mathematics,
then I fancy that it would be with a rather strange
and primitive freshness, like that of seeing the first flower
or even the first fairy, that we should behold afar off, at
the end of that telescopic perspective, the figure of the
Dancing Faun.

Therefore does a little fear fall upon me, over our own
satiety and restlessness in the presence of the great works
of the past. I am not sure there is not something thank-
less, as well as thoughtless, about a world which only
tosses and struggles because it is weighed down with too
much beauty and bounty, crushed with too much culture
and stunned with the weight of too many masterpieces.
I am not superstitious about these things; still less am I

Puritan or Manichæan; but I should not find it quite incredible if a wise man said that the cure for our trouble is to fast from statues and pictures and wait hopefully for an æon or two in a bare wilderness or before a blank wall. But in these fancies too there is danger of exaggeration and heresy, and upon the heresy of the Iconoclasts, I have already explained that I am entirely on the side of St. John Lateran and the Pope.

Before leaving St. John Lateran and the subject of such classical Christian churches, it will be well to add that what is really to be said for them, and what I have here attempted to say, does not (in my judgment) get rid altogether of the real criticism, which remained true however often Ruskin repeated it; that this art does express something, but that the something is not the religious sentiment, certainly not the Christian sentiment. They are a witness to the work religion has done for the world, to the common sense of the Catholic Church in using and moulding the materials of this earth; to the needs of all normal people; to the desire of all nations; to all that huge and human and colossal compliment which prigs and Puritans and Manichees and mystics with myopic eyes and thin noses pay to Catholicism when they say it is Pagan. But it does not seem to me specially designed to express the true mystical emotion any more than the false one. Only here and there, and as if by accident, you will find in Rome that sort of bright transparency, that sort of intensified innocence, that sort of delicate distortion, like the beautiful clumsiness of a child, that is suggestive in the Little Flowers of St. Francis or the coloured daylight of Chartres. Here and there a scrap of gay mosaic that seems to have stuck to the wall like a moth, though it has been there since the dim days of Byzantine Cæsars, will recall that nameless quality in the primitive which we can only insult by calling quaint. Here and there an old and dusty apse of gold, almost unnoticed like a quiet evening sky, will bring another tone into the riot of merely gilded things and remind us that behind the Renaissance was the childhood of the Church. But, broadly speaking, it is true that Rome is given over to another mood of manhood; and sometimes of excessively muscular manhood. Always, from its first tribal battles, a city of triumphs, it is the city of the Church in Triumph rather than of the Church in Ecstasy or the Church in Trial. To those who dislike the style intensely, this may be a good reason for turning their backs on the Holy City, but not a good reason for turning their backs on the Holy Catholic Church. The Church uses every style and will soon be using quite new styles. The Early Victorian æsthete venerated the Virgin of Raphael and was quite annoyed when the Late Victorian æsthete venerated the Virgin of Botticelli. But Eric Gill venerated the Virgin; and can therefore produce the Virgin of Eric Gill.

Of course, as the style of the Renaissance turned later

into what is sometimes called the Rococo, otherwise known as the Baroque, it was regarded even more as a bombshell; especially as it was spread by the Jesuits, who were credited with consistent readiness to throw a bomb. To say the least, this later caricature of classic architecture does sometimes remind the sensitive of a display of fireworks. There has recently been a fashion through which it seems likely to be as much overrated as it was once underrated. But I am only indirectly interested to decide these technical questions of art, in so far as they throw a light on the moral and political forces in the story of Rome. And it is quite obvious that the real objection to Baroque is a moral as well as a technical objection. It is bound up with a certain sincere desire for greater simplicity and directness in religion; with a sentiment that is sometimes mediæval and sometimes rather Puritan.

The Puritan before Ruskin wanted his buildings flat and classic and considered Gothic a sinful riot of ritualism. The Puritan after Ruskin wants his buildings Gothic and considers the classic not flat but florid, a sinful riot of Renaissance heathenism. He is perhaps not very consistent in his course, but he is in his way consistent in his object; and especially in his objection. What he objects to is what I should call Catholic culture and he would call Popish Paganism. In plain words, the real question that is raised by Renaissance and especially Rococo art is not an artistic question but a religious question; the old religious question of Protestant protests against Catholic ornament or display. It would be absurd for me to pretend that I am impartial on the point; but I fancy I am rather more capable of seeing both sides of it than is generally supposed by those of the other side. Catholic history contains much more of Protestantism than Protestant history does of Catholicism.

I can imagine some primitive figure like St. Peter, standing at the very first foundations of Christianity, in serious reflection, and indeed in reasonable doubt, about this question of whether the religion should or should not have a ritual like that of the Pagan religions. In fact some of the first Councils did really stand wavering thus; and the "images" which are now so much the mark, and especially the mock of Catholicism were taken out of their niches and put back again through a long period of simple and sincere hesitation. I think it is true that the Catholic faith might have scored in some ways if it had remained absolutely austere and unworldly; as poor as the birth in the Stable; as naked as the victim on the Cross. But I think a thousand times more certainly that *unless* it could have been kept at the last extreme of severity, it was right to rush to the last extremes of splendour. It was charged with something too great for mankind; it had to express something that can never be expressed, but which can only be faintly indicated by something startlingly plain or startlingly beautiful. It can be weakly suggested by the thirst and desolation of the desert, which seems to extort the cry of prophecy like a cry of pain. It can also be feebly hinted at by ten thousand trumpets blaring before a golden throne; robes of angry crimson or peacock fans unfolding the hundredfold eyes of night. But a religion that merely dresses for church as it dresses for dinner, a religion that merely prays into a top-hat and calls a suit of funeral black its Sunday best—that does not express what is expressed either by a hermit or a hierarchy; that does not express anything, except that its followers would have been equally contented with anything else. Whatever it is, the Church of Christ must not merely be what some of my Anglican friends used humorously to call Mod. High. It must be very high, like the spire of Cologne Cathedral or the tower of Salisbury; or else it must be very low, like the Catacombs or the Cave of Bethlehem. St. Francis is the Mirror of Christ and is ragged and barefoot with bleeding hands and feet. And the Pope is the Vicar of Christ and when he goes splendid in white and silver and gold, with the ostrich plumes and the peacock fans borne before him, he is only making the approximate attempt that every sort of picture makes, to symbolize a sort of vision. But a bland and prosperous parson in a dog collar, a little supercilious since being made an Archdeacon or a Rural Dean, he (though his counterpart exists in all religions) does not in any sort of way suggest that religion is at all remarkable. He ought either to be poorer in the practice of his religion or else richer in his expression of it. I do not mean, of course, that as an individual he is under any direct moral obligation to do otherwise than as he does in his circumstances and with his lights. But I am talking not about normal morals, but about the inadequate expression of an abnormal magnificence. For that purpose he should either be in a hovel such as covered the humility of Christ or else in a palace painted like the heavens that show forth the glory of God. I do not think, therefore, that the Papacy was wrong when, having once decided to meet human nature on the subject of ceremonial, it made it a very gorgeous ceremonial. I can see no good at all in it having made it a mean or doubtful or third-rate or threadbare ceremonial. But I can quite imagine the first of the Popes wondering whether it would not be more sublime to do without ceremonial altogether. And the only answer to that is the deepest answer of all, which comes to us in the words of the Mass like a movement of distant music, and to me always somehow suggests the innocent sway and rhythm of some dim antediluvian dance: "His delight is with the sons of men."

If you will, the Church is very willing to amuse us with picture-books because we cannot for long endure the strain of understanding everything by diagrams. But it is no very irrational part of human nature that she should try to make the pictures as good as possible, or sometimes even as gorgeous as possible. The alternative is the idea of no pictures, which, as we have seen, was essentially the ideal of Mahomet and the Iconoclasts. But even the case of the Moslem will itself serve to show that this ideal, of not expressing the divine at all, is really even more unattainable than that of expressing it adequately. Moslem art and culture have not really remained simply staring at the unity of God. Their instinct of self-expression has developed, only it has developed defectively. The banishment of the human face from their ornament did not make it less ornamental, but only less human. It did not leave the whole page a blank, or even limit it to the simplest and severest pattern. It only made it an unmeaning pattern, though it was also an involved one. It only made such art, magnificent indeed within its limitations, a labyrinth of headless serpents and eyeless fishes; of birds without motion and trees and flowers without root. The avoidance of idolatry has not led to simplicity, but merely to a more dead and dehumanized complexity. It is of course excellent, and even exquisite, of its kind, but it illustrates the fact that an ideal simplicity is not really maintained by any methods or by any men. The Arab out of the desert, crying the terrible truism that God is God, was of all men the wildest worshipper of simplicity. He came out of the golden glare of sand and sunlight, to proclaim that all religion must be as single as the sun and as naked as the drawn sword. Yet it is curious that even the most perfect sword blade of his own forging is famous for being "damascened"; and

[145]

that the one word which art has gathered from the Arab is Arabesque.

The point is here that Rome had to decide whether it would express the simplicity of Christ in simplicity or the glory of God in glory. Granted the latter, though I do not care for all the manifestations of it, I think it was right to make the glorification very glorious. In a hundred human and ordinary things the Church is very human and ordinary; her common sense completely accepts the medium or centre of gravity of Aristotle; the true doctrine of the golden mean. But in this special matter of expressing a spiritual prodigy, she was right not to go by the golden mean but rather by the golden extravagance. That ground is not so much the *via media* as the place where extremes meet. In this matter it is really all or nothing, and the only outrage is mediocrity. When it comes to the reaction to a revolution, to the result or effect of a miracle, to the attempt to utter something ultimately unutterable, the expressions of it must be in extremes; and even in opposite extremes. So in such a moment a man would either be struck silent or cry aloud; so under such a visitation men would either spring to their feet or fall on their faces. It is exactly the intermediate shade of refined hesitation that would really be vulgar; more vulgar than anything that is merely loud. To see a man rise from the dead and say "Dear me!" is worse than to say "Good God!" or to say nothing. Anyhow, anybody with any sort of instinct of art or letters in him will see in such things the case for extremes or even extravagances. A startling truth might be symbolized by pointing to a stone by the roadside or by building a tower of brass that seemed to break the clouds in the sky; but not by building a post of brass and making it a little shorter to save the expense. Epics could be written about a loose pebble or a large pyramid; but not about a small pyramid in a small front garden in Clapham. When we first see the monuments of Papal Rome, we may perhaps think the pyramid is rather too large; we may think that the brazen tower is rather too brazen. There is truth in the impression; for mortal motives are mixed, and there were impurities in the devotion as well as the decoration. But the evil was not in feeling that the tower could not be too high or the tomb too enduring; and the evil, I may add, was not in this case avoided by cautiously avoiding the good. Indeed those in other places who did avoid the good did not avoid the evil. The contemporaries of the Italian classicists, though in another way from the Arab Iconoclasts, illustrated the problem I mean; that there are a great many other ways in which complexity can return. Simplicity is not so simple as it looks.

Wherever there is pomp there is some peril of pomposity. But it is only fair to remember that most rebels against it have not ultimately avoided pomposity, even when they avoided pomp. When we see the Roman churches of the Baroque period, especially of the later seventeenth and early eighteenth centuries, we naturally feel a revulsion against them, because of something overloaded in their magnificence and something garish in their very gaiety. We rightly rebel against something that is meant to be glorious, and is often only vainglorious. But, as I say, it is only just to remember what has in history been the real alternative. If it were anything so simple as a choice between simplicity and luxury, the world, to say nothing of the Church, would never have made these brilliant blunders on quite so large a scale. If organized Christianity could at any moment choose between Francis Bernadone the beggar and Alexander Borgia the Pope, none of us would in that sense be Papists. If every age could turn at once either to Giotto the shepherd or to Bandinelli the blatant and swaggering courtier of the Renaissance, there would not be much hesitation in any age; not even the age of the Renaissance. But things are not so simple as that. Those who walk haughtily out of the Church of Rome, or even out of the churches of Rome (which is an uncommonly different thing) must walk somewhere and build something; they will probably build more churches, or possibly more chapels. But they also will take on in time an inevitable routine and respectability. They also will have their ritual, though it is a duller ritual; they also will have their conservatism, though they will have less interesting things to conserve. And we can see this at once if we glance at the powerful Protestant churches flourishing in the same

period as the Baroque in Rome; the churches of England
or Holland or the German States, with their royal patronage or their commercial wealth. They have the same
turgid touch of the time, but in a gloomier and less genial
fashion; like a French funeral compared with a French
fête. The memory of them is a sort of nightmare of dark
cherubim made of black marble instead of white. The
name of religion in the eighteenth century of Erastian
England does not call up a vision of Primitive Christianity. It calls up a vision of bishops in big wigs and belly-
ing black robes or lawn sleeves, their draperies overflow-
ing, we might almost say boiling over, the carved pulpits
and lowering galleries of the churches of their time; the
strictly classified pews, the huge exclusive volumes; the
heavy indigestible decoration. It is a religious age remembered rather by the beadle than the bishop. It was hardly
an age that had avoided pomposity by avoiding pomp.
It had only given to its pomp something indescribably
sulky and swollen-headed which is not really present in
the crazy confectionery of white and gold to be found in
the worst of the Rococo of the South. Indeed, if there was
a little less pomp, there was a little more pride. The
swagger was more in the soul, and especially in the mind.
That fashion was quite as florid; if it was florid in its
eloquence rather than its elegant accessories. That fashion
was quite as self-important; and indeed the importance
was more entirely in the self.

At least in the Roman churches there is something better than what was called Roman luxury; there is also what may be called Latin levity. For levity is not to be confounded with frivolity; certainly not with mere superficiality. There is a sort of sacred levity that is not inappropriately represented in saints rising, and even rushing, out of the grave, or angels soaring and sweeping into the sky. There is really some analogy between levity and levitation. There is at least a true touch of the Christian miracle in any sort of defiance of gravitation, which in every sense is associated with quite the wrong sort of gravity. To some these Baroque extravagances are even ghastly; but they are not gloomy. These shattering explosions of porphyry and gold, with their shafts of solid sunshine and their bubbles of buoyant cloud, are at least expressions of life and not of death; and are not entirely unworthy of this our recurrent theme of resurrection.

Most of the modern critics have made a great hash of the subject of religious art. First, because they cannot bring themselves to believe that it is theological art. And second because nobody ever told them how wide and many-sided and sympathetic a thing theology is; so long as it is the right theology. They have made the Christian artists, especially of Italy, differ from each other much more than they did; or rather not differ as they did, as artists and therefore as individuals, but differ as hopelessly as the hopeless modern philosophies differ. That is because they do not know the nature of the older philosophy, and do not know that there is room in it for all sorts of differences of temper and tone. To take one instance at random; Pater and the Pagans of our time talked of the sadness of Botticelli as if it were merely heathen or half-heathen because his angels look as wistful and unsatisfied as his graces; or the same cadaverous light falls on the Virgin as on the Venus. They simply did not happen to know that this is one aspect of Catholic theology; just as the most majestic *Mater Triumphalis,* stiff with Byzantine gold, is another aspect of it. It is an entirely Catholic sentiment that Mary is the second Eve and in that sense the second Venus; and that she feels the full pathos of the human fall and the fruitless but tireless search for a heathen happiness. She knows that pagan passion is beautiful, and she certainly knows that it is sad. Botticelli did not have to wait for Swinburne to feel all that; it is in the Creed. Then the modern critic will turn to somebody else and find something gloomy and violent in Michael Angelo and perhaps call *that* heathen; though it is exactly what a heathen would call gloomy and violent in Dante. The Faith faces every possible way, so far as angle and attitude to life is concerned; and there is no artistic style it cannot use. The jewel has a hundred facets, and reflects every colour and corner of the sky; but that does not mean that it wavers or wobbles; and those who would break it find it the hardest stone in the world.

It is necessary to grasp this, especially when we come upon an angle or attitude that we do not happen to like; as is the case with a multitude of northern people, living in the Ruskinian tradition, when they first see the Baroque; especially such boiling and foaming masses of the Baroque as bubble up from the very depths of Rome. I see that Mr. Karel Capek has written a most amusing and disarming little book about Italy, and among other foreign critics I think he is a thousand times more likely to be right because he continually confesses that he may be wrong. This attitude is so startling in an art critic, that I hail it with the veneration due to something great and heroic; and all the more so because I think he *is* wrong. He thinks that Christianity died with the Gothic and the Byzantine and that Catholicism, something different and practically Pagan, came in with the classical and the florid. There are a hundred answers to this; over and above an obvious query about Catholicism only beginning about the same time as Protestantism. Perhaps the shortest answer is to point out that the very period which plastered all the churches with naked cherubim and saints looking like sun-gods was the period that produced some of the most sensitive and humble and sympathetic of all the great Christians of history; that people like St. Vincent de Paul and St. Francis of Sales and St. Theresa walked in some such wilderness of white new marble and glaring tropic gold; their souls as delicate and transparent and tenderly coloured as any window of the

Middle Ages. The real explanation is not that they thought so much more of gold and marble, but that they thought so much less of them.

Christianity or Catholicism (and, with best wishes to Mr. Capek, they are not different) is something more than a mood. It is something more like an event; an event like a baby being born in a family. The parents know they will have hundreds of moods about the baby; ranging from something approaching idolatry to something drifting towards infanticide. But the fact is not altered, and other things, including moods, are adjusted to the fact. There can be all sorts of discussions in the family about the best style of toys for the baby; just as there are all sorts of discussions about the best style of art for the Church. There is a Golliwog School as there is a Gothic School; there are people who do not feel a wax doll from the Lowther Arcade as too florid or foolish, just as there are people who do not feel a Madonna of Murillo as too like a wax doll from the Lowther Arcade. There are others who would have every puppet in the nursery as perfect in form and balance as a Greek god in a temple; like that little figure of the Flying Mercury which was knocked off a motor-car in one of Mr. Wells's novels and picked up by a child, who preferred it to all his Punches and Teddy Bears. There is an endless and equal quarrel between the classic and the fantastic. It can always be said that reason and order are better than unreason and anarchy; and answered that there lies beyond our reason a world of wilder and more wonderful mysteries; and answered again that pure harmony is really the same as perfect liberty; and answered yet again that a more perfect liberty would seem to our limited vision imperfect. It is quite true, on the one hand, that the straight limbs of the Greek hero, or even the straight lines of the stiff Egyptian god, may be in truth a still whirlwind of perfect motion and energy. It is true again that there is something in us at once antic and domestic. Something for which a thing is not quite familiar unless it is a little outlandish. Something that is more at home with the goblins than the gods. That dispute can rage round the dolls of the nursery as round the idols of the temple. But those of us who are really concerned to apply it to the nursery or the temple do not really treat the differences as differences of deep loyalty or allegiance; they are a matter of means and not of ends. We, in the sense of those whose allegiance is the same as mine, do not feel about these schools of taste as the modern critics imagine, when they treat them as schools of thought. We like the doll that is as graceful as a dryad or the golliwog that is as hideous as a gargoyle. We pit them against each other and urge that this or that will be the more educational emblem; but we are not in the last resort thinking about these things. We are not merely comparing pleasures or merely pleasing ourselves; for to us a child is born.

This is what a man must understand first in contemplating the bold historic experiment of the Baroque. For the Church it was a very bold experiment; and, as I note elsewhere, it was by no means the first or last of such bold experiments. The Catholic Church, so often noted for its sleepy and hoary antiquity, has again and again been in the very vanguard of an advancing and changing world; and it is part of the joke that she has always suffered for it at the next change. She had filled the world with too many vigorous masterpieces when they were in the fashion; so there are too many of them to be pointed at as old-fashioned. So it was with the Aristotelian logic of the Middle Ages; when men produced so much logic that it came at last to choke up the path of progress like lumber. So it was with the classical revival of the Renaissance; when it produced so much classical sculpture and statuary as to choke up the streets of Rome like a barricade of colonnades and fountains or an obstacle-race of statues and shrines. Those who do not like it need not look at it; those who do like it will probably admit that there is rather too much of it. But at least let them remember that it was because the Church did move with the times that she has so entrenched and entangled herself in the memorials of the times. Indeed Rome is almost like somebody caught in the act of "moving," hemmed in by boxes and baggage.

I say that a man who would begin to be reconciled to this Rococo sequel of the Renaissance must first remember that it was a means to an end, like a doll for a child. It was a new doll but not a new child; and the child is more important than the doll. If we think of it in this way, we shall have the proportion and emphasis right, even if we continue to think it is an overdressed and tawdry doll, much inferior to the hard Dutch Doll of the Primitives. But indeed the infantile parallel applies even more in detail. When I want, as an old mediævalist, to force myself to be fair to the Baroque, I find that the most sympathetic medium is to take a pencil, especially one or two coloured pencils, and let the point wander over the paper in dashing and sprawling designs such as might be made for the back scenes of a child's toy theatre. In fact when people complain that this style is theatrical, they are not wrong and not necessarily hostile. There is in all the churches, that look like palaces, a broad quality of scene-painting; there is also something like a quality of scene-shifting. Many of them have been removed and recast and raised again as by the gestures of a gigantic stage carpenter. But there is nothing necessarily false in this nameless air of being, not even palaces, but rather the pavilions of a moving pageant of progress. All that is necessary is to put ourselves, as a child would do, in sympathy with that sort of scenery. Preferably, as I say, to take a pencil and design that sort of scenery. The draughtsman will find that the crayon moves quite swiftly and naturally to create such forms, if he does not bother about whether they belong to any school of architecture. For the truth is that they are not architecture but draughtsmanship, like the swirl of flying figures sketched on the Sistine Chapel. I quite concede that there is something strictly more sincere in the architecture which is architecture, and which is especially building. Mr. Eric Gill once said that in sculpture a man must be a stone man, but the sort of man that God would have made if he had used stone. It is the glory of the great Gothic and the best Romanesque that no liveliness of detail ever makes us forget that the house of God is still a house, and a house made of stone. I agree that the Baroque does not do this; it is rather the work of a magician drawing pictures in the air. He sweeps up his hand and makes the curve of a cloud, he cleaves it and lets forth a shaft of sun. It is not real cloud or real sun, and does not pretend to be; but it does, as it were, pretend to pretend. It is theatrical; but a theatrical performance is not a falsehood, for it does not profess to be a fact. Still, there is a difference; it does not really look like cloud or sunshine, but then it does not really look like plaster or timber. It does not really look like what it really is. That does, I think, mean a deep and real separation from the Stone House or the Stone Man. . . . But what does it matter, so long as the child is pleased?

All churches are built to please the Child in heaven; but these churches were rather specially built to please the children of men. Perhaps, in spite of the apparent sophistication of the style and the period, they were in a peculiar sense addressed to the child in man. And that is why they remind me of the bold scenery of a panto-

mime or a toy-theatre, and even St. Peter's Dome sometimes looks like Aladdin's Palace. There really were historical and political reasons. This riot is the Counter-Reformation; the great raid made by Rome to recapture
her popularity in the lost provinces and among the alien-
ated groups. If in this style there is something explosive,
if there is something which some not unnaturally call
vulgar, it is partly because the Church is deliberately playing the demagogue. I think it was Monsignor Benson
who pointed out that, with all the tenderness of the
Gothic churches, there is more uninterrupted access to
the altar in the Renaissance shrines; and that is connected
with the sort of thing that the Counter-Reformation,
whatever its faults, really did do. It flung open the gates.
No longer counting on the devout populace to wait outside, it called on the doubtful populace to come in and
see. It at once defied and implored the world. I have said
that some of the Renaissance statues in St. Peter's are
flowing with lines that are akin to rhetoric. It may fairly
be said of some of the Baroque effects in churches that
they are akin to tub-thumping. All this men will blame
or praise or pardon, according to their tastes or tempera-
ments; but it will be well for them first of all to understand.

In short the Counter-Reformation, which used the
Baroque like a blazon or a blare of trumpets, was but another example of the special sort of energy we have seen
everywhere in this history; the energy of resurrection. It

was the return of the dead or at least of the defeated; the counter-attack of the conquered; the surprise attack made by those supposed to have been disarmed. If some of the strokes of this surprise attack are a little surprising, we need not in our turn be surprised. In fact the Baroque effects in Rome have really rather a suggestion of somebody storming the high places, and even the holy places of the city; like that kingdom which the violent take by storm. It is really rather as if men were setting stone and brass on fire, or rolling the reeling columns in smoke, or pouring down molten marble as the old fighters poured down melted lead. The Church is using, and using up, the materials of the world, burning up gold and gorgeous substances in one furious battle for popularity and public appeal; and those who like it least should look upon it as a battle-field; and remember that the battle was won. For since the seventeenth century Popes and the Society of Jesus splashed all Europe with this splendid vulgarity, there has never been any question of their religion really disappearing among the populace of the Latin and the old Catholic lands. Whatever our own beliefs or unbeliefs, we shall not understand the human history of the thing, until we realize that what many not unreasonably regard as the decay of art was the resurrection of religion. It may be that a degenerate art was used recklessly for a resurrected religion, though there may be two opinions even about the degeneration. It is often said, for instance, that the Jesuit use of the genius of Rubens in itself marked a degeneracy from the most sincere Christian art. I need not discuss that here. But, after all, what sort of a decay is it which in corruption breeds not worms but giants; and what sort of strength of which Rubens was the weakness and the decline?

To sum up; Baroque architecture is not architecture, but it is art. It is rather as if I, for one, should say that Walt Whitman's poetry is not poetry, but it is literature. Baroque architecture seems to me to belong rather to the art of painting, and especially, as I have said, of scene-painting. It is in fact simply painting a Renaissance picture in three dimensions instead of two. It is attempting to give solidity and substance to those dreams of Rococo curve and colour which we all recognize, without much resentment, in the corresponding school of pictures. A column and a cloud and a sunburst and a careering seraph are normal enough in any number of pictures; but here they are deliberately turned into furniture. They are given thickness and stereoscopic solidity and all that is necessary for seeing them from all sides like a statue. But a cloud and a sunburst and a seraph are not *building;* they could not possibly build anything or assist in the building of anything, and as a matter of fact they are not meant to. It may have been an exaggeration to call them false, for they were not meant to deceive, any more than they were meant to construct. But it is not an exaggeration to call them sensational, for they were meant to make a sensation and not to make a building. When all this was allowed for, we can enjoy what is really fascinating and stimulating in such fancies, as we should in our childhood have enjoyed a transformation scene in a pantomime; and only a too sensitive reverence will be very much annoyed if the transformation is called a transfiguration. But there does remain a vast distance between that sort of thing and the strong craftsmanship, that can make a thing ornamental in the very act of making it useful. The mediæval tradition is still superior in so far that it can make a beautiful tool, which is not merely a pantomime sceptre or a property sword. There is a simpler and nobler sort of work, which has from the beginning made a boat beautiful because it could float and a building beautiful because it can stand. But Rome is not the place where one can reasonably look for such simplicities. By the very nature of its complex story, it has every virtue except simplicity.

I have treated this matter of Renaissance art and its sequel at some length and yet insufficiently; first because I do not claim the right to treat it technically; and second because I do claim the right to treat it more or less morally. Never was art less unmoral than the art discussed here. Never was art less for art's sake than that which was done in Rome by some of the greatest artists of the world. The whole matter was not only moral but theological; and any treatment of that is always insufficient. But I am very glad that I have ventured to talk like a

Christian and not a cultured person; that I have borne some sort of testimony to the things to which these men really wished to testify; and that I have unburdened my mind of an unaffected and even affectionate contempt for the numerous varieties of fool who think that the Renaissance was Pagan; that Pan is living but that Christ is dead. I have said what I think of them and got it off my mind. I arise more cheerful, like the Obelisk.

V · THE RETURN OF THE ROMANS

I happen to be so constituted that I can enjoy almost any weather, except what is called glorious weather. But I also have a dim feeling of resentment when this sort of weather is alone accounted glorious. I can understand that the word might not naturally be applied to the condition of climate I happen to enjoy most; which is, broadly speaking, the climate of my own country. It is the sort of cool and brisk grey weather which is felt as appropriate to early winter or very early spring; and the complaint of my ungrateful countrymen merely consists of saying that it is quite as common in summer and appears to last all the year round. But I can quite understand that it costs them an effort to call it glorious. But one season, like one star, differs from another in glory; and I do not admit that the only star is that which we call the sun. Similarly, I know not why even Pagans, in this once Pagan city, should reserve all their worship for Apollo; or forget that there is a planet called Jupiter in the skies or a god called Jupiter on the Capitol. My experience of weather in Rome, in the late autumn, is that

it is emphatically glorious weather, in the sense of god-
like weather but not only because Phœbus still blazes
from the firmament, but also because Jove can still thun-
der from the rock. Rain in Rome is a truly glorious thing.
I do not wonder that they worshipped Jupiter under the
name of Jupiter Pluvius. It is at the opposite extreme
from the rain that hangs about indecisively over the Atlantic islands. It is the reverse of that Celtic Twilight the
Scots call soft weather. Here, even in the heart of a great
city, rain while it lasts is exceedingly hard weather. It
rings on all the stone and metal like something metallic;
like something harder than hail. One might easily
imagine that it was really a crash of thunderbolts, hurled
by the old heathen god from his Capitoline throne; by
that dark and mysterious Sky-Father to whom, after every
victory, the Romans returned. Indeed the vivid and sometimes abrupt alternations of late but strong sunshine with
storm and rain and even cold may throw some light, for
all I know, on those endless myths of the men of the
Mediterranean about celestial powers in conflict and the
rivalry of the gods. But there is a further effect of these
conditions which has a closer reference to the history of
Rome. I do not need to be told that the sky is astonishing everywhere and should alone keep all men from materialism or indifference; that sunsets purple with passion
illuminate Pimlico or apocalyptic daybreaks cry aloud
and in vain to West Ealing. But, being myself much
travelled in these realms of gold, I have never for some

[166]

reason seen a modern city in which the sky seemed so continuously significant as in Rome. It may be connected, like most Roman things, with some reading of the traditional into the actual. But I do not think this is entirely the case. There are hours of evening when a red sunset stands behind the dome of St. Peter's like a Cardinal in all his robes, unwrinkled, unstained, untouched by any spot of cloud, the sky more solid than the land. There are other times when the sky seems filled with fragments, jagged and detached, as if another world had been broken in space. And it is impossible not to recall at such a moment the long inheritance of legend which has so repeatedly accompanied the Roman story with a story of signs in heaven; or to forget the meteors that blazed forth the death of Cæsar or that rending of the secret skies, which was seen by the Evangelist above the City of the Seven Hills.

I was leaning over the wall of the Pincio Gardens, and below me there was nothing but a fall of steps and a fringe of palm-trees, deserted except for one of the ordinary civic guards standing and gazing across the valley. There had recently been a spouting storm of rain and the whole scene was bright with the tiny mirrors of water. But the sky was still filled with floating wrecks of cloud lit from below by the last light from the now wan and lurid day. The hot and heavy storm that hangs indecisively above Rome in autumn took the form, for the moment, of something like a strange configuration of the sky; and, for some unreasonable reason, it was behind this, and not more solemn scenes and figures, that there seemed to pass vaguely an emblematic pageant of the past. To say that in such a reverie the dreamer saw the long story of Rome would naturally be a lie; like the well-established lie about the retrospect of the drowning man, which no properly drowned man has ever come back either to claim or contradict. But the drowning man, like the dreaming man, may possibly see what we all see in moments of surprise or abstraction or driving haste; symbolic shapes like mere scraps taken at random and referring in some fashion to a longer catalogue. And it was at that moment, and in that lurid dusk, for some reason that I fancied I saw disconnected and dreadful things that had happened long ago appearing in the sky like omens; and especially those that had really been seen, as old traditions told, against the sky: the black birds of aboriginal augury and the shield falling from heaven: and the starry signs of evil which Livy recorded; and the spear of Hannibal hurtling above Rome and hung in heaven like one of the thunderbolts of Jove; and the ensigns going up the rock of the Capitol and that yellow giant burning in the sun that was the colossal figure of the greatest of earthly tyrants; and high in heaven the holy place whose name alone suggests a cloudy altar in the sky and Simon the Magician hung in the void like a star and falling like a stone; and in the long battering sieges the great gesturing statues of the Cæsars hurled through the sky like huge stone arrows upon the heads of the Goths; and so through a thousand stages of a story that has been one everlasting storm. For at every stage of the story of Rome, Pagan and Christian, it has been accompanied, men say, by signs in heaven; but I know not why they should have thus crowded upon my own fancy in that casual connection.

Every one knows how in such a sky, which is sown with shards and shattered fragments of cloud, it is easy to fancy half a hundred figures or significant shapes, sometimes of almost incredible solidity and similarity; and it was not unnatural to find in such a cloudland the flying wizard or the falling god. All the clouds were drifting very slowly across the dome, but as I looked at one small dark clot of cloud, I saw with a subconscious thrill that it was moving faster than the rest. Indeed it was soon moving like an arrow; and I saw that it was an aeroplane. And something in this now familiar object seemed new and unfamiliar, as it rose through the clearing skies beyond the last rags of the storm. This Icarus was after all the last phase of Italy and the end of the long string of portents, that ended with the flying ship as it began with the falling shield. And there swept through my mind as with a rush of such winged chariots, the tales of Fiume and the fight; and over Austria the avenging aviators and all that Mr. Squire has truly called the demoniacal courage of D'Annunzio. Nobody can doubt that Italy of the ages is alive, who remembers the legend that is alive with eagles, and the strong riders of the Renaissance, and then thinks of that wild poet pouring fire from heaven; a man dangerous in peace and war. We need not accept all aspects of such a man, any more than of Benvenuto Cellini; but the man is the same and is still alive. And from this last of the signs in heaven my mind went slowly backwards to the vast and titanic tragedy which occasioned all such courage, and out of which at last Italy has come transfigured. I thought of my own country and the heroic and heartening part she played in the Great War; and the strange taste for unheroic and disheartening literature that has since been cultivated in her reading public. And as I would rather rejoice with the triumph of Italians than defile myself with the belated despair of German Jews, I turned to the consideration of that colossal combat; and especially of the reverberations of it in the hills of Rome.

What *was* the Great War? There are broadly four fundamental theories which make some sort of historical sense, apart from newspaper nonsense. It will be well to state them first as clearly and fairly as possible; if sense and not nonsense is to direct our view of post-war Italy. Of these four theories I myself hold the fourth. I know it is the one that is least held and least understood. I am prepared to prove here that it is the only one which makes any sense of what has actually happened.

The first interpretation is roughly that of the rivalry of the British Empire and the German Empire. There is up to a point, of course, a truth in this. For some time past there had been between the Prussian and the British systems a curious rage of imitation; an acrid anger of mutual admiration. There was so complete an agreement that every shrewd person knew that it would end in disagreement. England had been in a phase of boasting about her Empire and Germany in a phase of envying that Empire. Both agreed that possessing colonies of a certain sort, commerce of a certain sort, and naval strength of a certain sort, were the things to be envied. There was another side to the mutual flattery, which led to the mutual fury; and I shall mention it in a moment. But it is well to realize that there went along with all the arrogance of Prussia a queer sort of barbarous admiration for the modern Imperialism of Great Britain. The ordinary German was taught to reconcile his arrogance with his admiration by means of the silly schoolmaster's fairy-tale about the Teutonic Race. The Englishman and the German were brothers; like Cain and Abel. That was one theory of the primary passions of the War. But apart from anthropological antics about Teutonism, it is well to note that Prussia had from of old this antic of imitation. Frederick the Great was a French king though a Prussian squire. His whole plan of palace, camp and city was on the French pattern; he did not even speak German. Just as Frederick fought the French from bitter admiration of their army, so William fought the British from bitter admiration of their navy. In both cases there was the same foreign fashion inflaming local ambition. The favourite author of Wilhelm the Second was Kipling; just as the favourite author of Frederick the Second was Voltaire. The world has grown steadily less and less international (though the internationalists are vexed when told so) and it was impossible for the Kaiser to ask Mr. Kipling to come and live at his palace or even in his kingdom, as Frederick had asked Voltaire. The Kaiser had to be content with the estimable Mr. Houston Stewart Chamberlain, whom most of us (possibly excepting Dean Inge) are less likely to miss. But there was this element of fierce flattery, of hard and hostile plagiarism; and it must count for something. On the other side, even before the simple German had been taught to take the British Empire seriously, the equally simple Briton had been taught to take the Germanic Race seriously. In all the schools and universities Englishmen were taught to be proud of being Germans: actually, in so many words, of being a certain sort of Saxon. Everything German was held up to incessant admiration up to the very moment of the War. Some of us expected that if the English and the Germans went on admiring each other like this, there would certainly be war. We even endeavoured to introduce a little disagreement and difference, in the hope of keeping the peace. We tried to point out that the Englishman and the Prussian were really rather remote from each other, and might well go their very separate ways. We pointed out, for instance, that even the English weakness, the excessive worship of the gentleman, cut him off from the North German; for the Prussian aristocrat, in the English sense, is not a gentleman at all. He is on principle stiff, stingy and brutal, instead of being genial, generous and patronizing. Thus, we tenderly pointed out, there is a basic distinction even between a nation of snobs and a nation of serfs. With such soothing and reconciling words did we attempt to persuade the English and the Germans that they were not so frightfully similar as to be bound to kill each other; that there was quite enough contrast to allow them to live side by side in peace. But all such feeble reassurances were drowned in the deafening generalization about the Germanic Race; which was apparently the same as the Race for Empire. Everybody in England seemed ready for the first or Anglo-German theory of war; the theory of Rivalry. Rivalry is the war between two things, not because they are different but because they are alike.

Allowing reasonable weight to this first theory, we may pass on to the second. In this also there is a truth; indeed of the two I think it is the truer. Anyhow it is roughly this. So far from being a rivalry between two similar things, it was the recurrence of an unending duel between two deeply dissimilar things; popularly represented by the words French and German. It may reasonably be said that they are the only two things in Europe that have never been heartily friendly and at one. The English way of putting it is that the War was the return match for 1870. It is a very English way of putting it; for the sporting metaphor implies a geniality that is not German and a frivolity that is not French. The French way of putting it, we were always told, was to talk about *Revanche*. And this again was a very French way of putting it; for it was making it out much worse than it was. There is always in the Frenchman a touch of that bitterness that is bitter against itself; and he was quite ready to say he was only asking for revenge when in fact he was only asking for justice. If Prussia had defeated us and taken away Yorkshire and Lancashire to add to the German Empire, we should not have exposed ourselves to misunderstanding by asking for "revenge." There is in the same case, as part of the same spirit, the invariable habit of the French of talking more about their failures than their successes. It has been truly said "they are tenacious of the memory of defeats rather than victories." All French literature begins with a song of defeat, of the fall of Roland in the Pyrenean pass, and it is French art as much as any that has fixed in our imagination that figure who had a hundred blazing victories to his name, as if he rode huddled and frozen for ever on an endless road from Moscow. In this, as in the parallel passion for crying out against political betrayal, the French are for good and evil the very opposite of the English. The English do not lament over lost battles, for the simple reason that they are never allowed to hear of any. A Frenchman knows well enough what is meant by Agincourt or

Blenheim or Leipzig. "Waterloo" is the name of a whole long poem by Victor Hugo: and one of the lightest and most popular of the songs or jingles familiar to French children commemorates the fact that the great Duke of Marlborough goes to war. But say to an Englishman "Orleans; Steenkirk; Fontenoy; Turcoing; Toulon"; and no wrath will kindle in his eye, for he has never so much as heard of a single one of these English defeats. In this sense it is true that a tradition of *Revanche,* or the righting of old wrongs, counted for something in the European quarrel, and that the French would certainly have recovered the stolen French provinces whenever they could; and quite right too. According to this second theory, their diplomacy had been patiently, intelligently and intensely directed to this end; they had succeeded in obtaining first an alliance with Russia, and later an understanding with England; and that, even if the actual aggression came from Germany, it did not come until France had succeeded in encircling her with foes. This theory is true in the sense that France was probably the most fully conscious and concentrated and intellectually convinced of the Allies; and of all the millions of brave men of many bloods and creeds who perished in that awful depopulation, it was her sons who least doubted for what they died.

The third theory is more remote and in a sense more mysterious; and has the grave disadvantage of having little or nothing to do with us. According to this theory,

we of the West, the British and even the French, were
hanging onto the edge of the affair, almost like those
others of the East, the Japanese or the Sepoys. The centre
of the War was in the centre. It pivoted on the Central
Powers and the notion of Mittel-Europa; or, in other
words, upon the war frontier between Austria and Russia.
It was the Slav against the Teuton; especially it was
Pan-Slavism against Pan-Germanism. For that reason, it
might well be said, the whole business began in the
Balkans. For that reason it began with a provocative ultimatum from Austria to Serbia. For that reason, it might
be argued, the civilized and patriotic state of Poland
stood somewhat detached and doubtful; treated best by
Austria and worst by Prussia. The Pole is the least Slav
of the Slavs. Anyhow, he is the least Pan-Slav of the
Slavs. He is a patriot on the Western pattern, and cares
about a nation and not a race. But over all the rest of
that vast inland continent were only vague and un-
charted realms of race and religion; but especially religion. And in a manner less clear-cut than the West understands, there stood facing each other two vast powers
or cultures; at the head of one of which stood, in the
main, the White Czar of all the Russias; and at the
head of the other the Emperor of that patchwork Empire held together by Vienna; the last of the Holy Roman
Empire, still claiming the crown of Charlemagne. It
might be an exaggeration to call it, as if out of some
page of Gibbon, a war between the Eastern and the

Western Cæsar. But it did count enormously in the matter that millions of those nomadic and nationless populations knew of no real difference, except that one followed the Byzantine and the other the Roman rite. Anyhow, that is roughly the third conception, and as I say, there is something in it, mysterious and for us hard to measure. For over everything connected with Russia or even the New Rome of Constantine, there is flung faint but vast, something that is not ourselves; the shadow of Asia.

I can believe in supernatural explanations, but not in unnatural natural explanations. I can accept a miracle if it is proved, or even sometimes when it is not proved; but I cannot accept an ordinary practical event which ought to be proved and is not even probable. I could believe that the unfortunate Archduke of Austria, who was a good man, saw visions of Our Lady on the morning when he was murdered. I could even believe that the aged Emperor of Austria, on the morning he sent the ultimatum to Serbia, was specially favoured by a materialization of his Guardian Angel, telling him not to be a fool. But I cannot with any ease believe that the Archduke put on his hat and began smoking a large cigar in the middle of Mass. And my faith fails me when I attempt to believe that the venerable Emperor attempted to stand on his head in order to receive the American Ambassador. These incidents are not miracles; they are within the material order of nature; they disturb no chemical principle, save in so far as turning somersaults is bad for the aged; but they are things that do not happen. And in the same way I do not and cannot believe that the Emperor of Austria, however aged or ill-advised, could possibly have signed the ultimatum to Serbia without knowing that it was at least twenty to one that it meant war with Russia. I do not believe that he or his counsellors, or any human beings, could in so violent a fashion have challenged the Slavs without knowing that they were challenging the Czar of all the Russias. I do not believe that they, or any human beings, would have challenged all the Russians without being absolutely certain that their action was backed up by their allies of all the Germanies. It was not a question of unfair terms of peace. What they forced upon the Serbs was war; with no thinkable alternative to war. To force such a war at all, upon the perilous peace of Europe, was for sane men to take the whole responsiblity of the whole huge catastrophe that actually followed. But if they had not only taken the responsibility to God and their fellow creatures of starting a European War, but also taken the responsibility to Austria of throwing her unsupported against Russia and all the Slavs, they would not have been even sane men, and hardly men at all. And, on the principle I have mentioned, I decline to believe that the two or three most manifestly rank and raving lunatics of the whole planet happened to have obtained the two or three chief political posts in Vienna by mere coincidence and purely natural causes.

I happen therefore to believe what I said, and what for five or six years all my countrymen said; that the whole story makes no sense unless Prussia was really prompting the War. The idea of Austria prompting Prussia, or pushing Prussia into anything that Prussia did not want, seems to me starkly crazy and incredible to anybody who knows what the balance of Europe has been ever since Sadowa and Sedan. For this reason I do not accept, at any rate in its fulness, what I may call the third or oriental theory of the War. I do not believe its ultimate origin was an antagonism to Slav Orthodoxy in Austria alone; because I do not believe that any such gigantic task would ever have been undertaken by Austria alone. And when we turn to the allies of Austria we turn again to the other explanations. We turn especially to the fourth explanation, which I have not yet given and which I shall now try to describe and defend.

This view was very little held, or at least very little emphasized in England. I do not remember any ordinary journalists except Mr. Belloc and my brother Cecil Chesterton and myself who insisted on it; though it was held by many learned men of a quieter sort, like Professor F. Y. Eccles, and could boast some inspiration in the past from so very human and virile a don as Sir Arthur Quiller-Couch. It was at least founded on the sort of view suggested by the latter in an admirable essay called "Antiquam Exquirite Matrem." But it was suggested more than once abroad, and perhaps nowhere better suggested than in two chance French phrases that I will quote here. They sum up this theory of the War for those who understand it; but in the present atmosphere I fear it may be necessary to explain it further. The first word was spoken when a French diplomatist said in the first days of military contact, "In every civilized land there goes up the ancient cry, 'Down with the Barbarians!'" And the other was spoken on the occasion of Italy's entrance to the War, I believe by the President of the French Senate: "As the old augurs watched the birds, we behold and hail, as an omen of victory, the flight of the Roman eagles."

The theory was fundamentally this; that what was wrong was that Europe was standing on its head. That is, its head was underneath and its heels were on top. The heels were beautifully booted and spurred and went through admirable demonstrations of kicking or goose-stepping in the void; they were excellent things in their way but they were not meant to be on top; they were not the sort of things to be trusted on top; and they were on top. Meanwhile the head of Europe, the natural spiritual and intellectual headship, was in the dust and even in the dirt; and continually being despised as dirty. That, we said, was a situation that was bound to produce some sort of revolt or reversal; and if people did not see it, it was because they had forgotten what that headship had always been, even to themselves as well as everybody else.

There is only one word to express it. There is mixed up in all this a queer importation from America; imported or exported like a very undesirable alien. It is not a fair sample of course. There is in the whole business of America a singular intellectual injustice; the republic that was made by recent and romantic pioneering has come to stand for standardization; the nation whose instinct was all for individualism for the insolent impersonality of the Trusts. And the nation which emerged late in history out of a civil war fought by enthusiastic volunteers has come, by a stupid accident, to be popularly associated with that sort of morality that is too proud to fight, but not too proud to foreclose. So the rest of the modern world receives in a very curious fashion the very dregs of the democratic experiment; and remains ignorant of a dozen great American orators in order to pick up and treasure some fragments of stale slang. And assuredly the very dregs of the dregs, which we have managed to lift or borrow from the very lowest level of American intelligence or unintelligence, is the now fairly common English fashion of using the word Dago.

The historical implications of this phrase are very amusing. The Dago, generally speaking, is a member of those darker races which have colonized South America and whose original breeding-ground is to be sought in the peninsulas of the Mediterranean. The chief characteristics of the Dago are knives, rags, romantic passions, reckless behaviour, garlic and guitars. With these things the beings in question create a perpetual disturbance quite out of proportion to their importance, or in other words to their wealth; and have been a terrible nuisance to the more solid communities who are acquainted with the Reign of Law. A considerable time ago, for instance, a gang of these desperadoes engaged in a desperate squabble with knives, after which one of them was left for dead and the rest were pursued by his friends with a typical vendetta. This sordid incident was exaggerated and made a subject for drama, or melodrama, until every child has been told that the name of the dead man was Julius Cæsar, and that the man who stabbed him made some rhetorical claim to be his friend. Other incidents equally squalid and sensational have unfortunately flattered the Dago vanity; some Dago from one of the dirty little islands seems to have run away and become a soldier, like so many ne'er-do-wells, and caused considerable excitement all over Europe until his criminal career ended in his being captured and sent to jail in St. Helena. There is another sordid story, on which we need not dwell, about a runaway sailor who advertised himself in a very vainglorious fashion and added insult to injury by actually discovering America. It is sometimes said unkindly that the discovery ought to have been hushed up. But it is only fair to say that it was another Dago who discovered Britain; and possibly that ought to have been hushed up too. It would certainly have been in better taste, if the Dagoes had hushed up all the things that they did in history; only if they had, there would not be very much history left. We need not linger on the unsavory theme; but talking about rags, it is enough to add that there was once one Dago at least who actually professed that he preferred to be poor. He lived in Assisi and Bishop Barnes does not think that his way of going on would be at all proper in Birmingham.

In short, if it were really necessary to regard the legend of the dirty and dingy Dago as a specimen of the new culture of the new world, I fear that most people who know anything of human history will continue to get their notions from the old world. And having found the legend so very inadequate in the case of the Dagoes of South Europe, they will perhaps even venture to doubt its infallible truth about the Dagoes of South America. Anyhow if all that is contemptible is a litter of little re-publics rocking with revolutions, they can extend that contempt to all Hellas in the age of Pericles and all Italy in the age of Dante.

In a word, it is all nonsense: inhuman unhistorical nonsense. For fully a thousand years, indeed up to what is relatively only the last few years, all the nations of the North lived cheerfully by a culture that had come from the South; and that culture had come from, or at any rate through, the old international realm of Rome. It had nothing to do with political submission to Rome; it long survived religious separation from Rome. It was not something that men were ashamed of, like enslavement. It was

[183]

something that men were proud of, like education. They were no more ashamed of it than Americans are ashamed of being white men from Europe, rather than black men from Africa or red men from America. They were no more insulted by it than a Christian is insulted by the existence of the Holy Land. It was something admitted and admired. Bayard was a Frenchman and Sir Philip Sidney was an Englishman and the Admirable Crichton was a Scotsman, and so on; and nobody doubted their loyalty to their own lands. But when these men were praised, the highest standard for praising them was to say they were as firm as Cato or as bold as Cæsar or as virtuous as Trajan. There was no other kind of praise, such as was afterwards invented to fit the Nordic fad about our unmixed descent from Hengist and Horsa. Bayard fought with his face turned towards Rome and Lucretia; Sidney's Arcadia was filled with the classic shepherds of Virgil. The Admirable Crichton was admirable because the Latins admired him when he talked Latin in Bologna and the schools of Italy. Nobody can read three pages of real English literature without knowing this fact. Shakespeare had small Latin and less Greek but plenty of Plutarch; and Hamlet, as well as Horatio, is really more the antique Roman than the Dane. But it is a complete mistake to suppose that this classical tradition was peculiar to classical scholars. It ran through the most popular and even the most vulgar things. Somebody wished to write a quite rowdy patriotic song, with the enlightening refrain of "Row-tow-tow-tow-tow," and the excellent but limited object of glorifying the British Grenadiers. And the instinctive way for him to begin, the only way he can begin, if he is to make a complimentary comparison, is to start with the classics. He records the unimpeachable fact that some talk of Alexander and some of Hercules; but nobody of Hengist—still less of "Hengst." Somebody else wanted to throw off an equally casual and probably convivial English song about England's patron saint and his fight with the dragon. His St. George is quite confined to England, not without rather insular jokes against Ireland. He obviously killed the dragon not at Ludd but at Ludgate Hill. But when the poet wants to prove that the English champion was really recognized among champions, his natural way is to write like this:

> Of the deeds done by old kings
> Is more than I can tell,
> And chiefly of the Romans,
> Who greatly did excel;
> Hannibal and Scipio
> Had many a bloody fight,
> And Orlando Furioso
> Was a very gallant knight.
> Romulus and Remus
> The town of Rome did build—
> But St. George, it was St. George
> That made the dragon for to yield.

[185]

That is the tradition, the purely popular tradition, that runs through a thousand things in English life and letters; and I have only taken two or three random instances where I could take two or three hundred. All over England, the little children of the villages and the slums could be heard singing, as the refrain of the ritual of an ancient game, "For we are the Romans."

That romance of Rome, as the international legend behind all the national legends, remained the chief reality of the world nearly down to our own time. As I say, it was a pride for Northerners as well as Southerners, for Protestants as well as Catholics; a truism for the French Revolution as much as for the Italian Renaissance. Then something began to happen, which has made all the mischief in modern Europe and ultimately made the Great War. As with most big and obvious things, it is hard to detect its dim beginning. Perhaps it began when the alliance failed against Frederick the Great. Perhaps it began when the alliance succeeded against Napoleon. The Industrial Revolution had a great deal to do with it; the expansion of a more Puritan England in America had perhaps as much; the commercial and colonial success of England had much, the temporary but rapid military success of Prussia had more. Anyhow, there entered the world a new notion, which may be called the notion of the New Nations. It was the idea that old centres like Rome were as dead as old cities like Nineveh, and that power was perpetually passing to other centres, always more novel

and generally more northern. Like all false generalizations, it could always quote a plausible chain of coincidences. Power had passed from Egypt to Greece, from
Greece to Rome, from Rome to Spain, from Spain to
France, from France to England, and now from England
to Germany or America, according as the philosopher
happened to be a Hun or a Yank. But the general notion
was that the new power was to be found in the north,
and especially in colder climates; though the time had
not yet come for Spitzbergen to conquer the world or for
the Eskimo to announce himself as the Superman.

The Nordic theory was supported by the Teutonic theory. Most of us were given a false moral ancestry like a
forged birth-certificate; a document in Double Dutch
which contradicted all our literature and living traditions. We were told that our culture came, not from the
Cross which everybody could see, but from the Hammer
of Thor which nobody had ever seen. We were told that
England began her life with the Vikings when it would
be truer to say that she escaped with her life by killing
the Vikings. All the natural flow of tradition from Rome
to the rest of the world was blocked and hidden; and a
counter-current set up suggesting that all generous im-
pulses had flowed from the Nordic barbarians, like
warm and genial currents flowing from the North Pole.
This was the view of history taught exclusively in my
youth to all the English, to nearly all the Americans and
naturally to all the Germans and Scandinavians. But after

the Prussian triumph over Paris, it overshadowed all
Europe and imposed itself to some extent on the South;
at least in a negative sense of inferiority or failure. In a
word, something had broken or failed in the mind of the
citizen of Europe; and what was gone was the respect for
Rome. In the world of the imagination Rome was being
treated, not only as a ruin but as a rubbish-heap; though
a rubbish-heap poked and prodded and pottered over by
æsthetes as well as vandals. The Mediterranean was no
longer the Central Sea. It was a more or less ornamental
pond in the back-garden that nobody need look at. The
Latins were a sort of luxurious and yet impecunious
remnant left over from a lazier age and incapable of
effort or efficiency; capable only of gesticulating over
organs and ice-cream carts. This was the universal tone
implied by talk and teaching in the nineteenth century;
I was brought up in the middle of it and I know. It was
general, it was systematic, it was specially proud of being
scientific. And every reflective man, every traditional
man, every true European, every true Englishman who
knew what the life had been in English letters and ideas,
knew in his bones that it was all wrong.

It could not be true that our mother was so base a wanton; that what had borne us was so barren, that what had
made us was so uncreative; that what had seemed most
great to all our greatest countrymen could be of a sort
to seem small to a few half-baked Junkers in Berlin. It
was all wrong; the boots were on top of the brains; the

boots were trampling out the brains; the barbarians were despising their teachers and, while they did, they could never be taught. It was this feeling of reaction against the *nouveau riche* of Europe, against the Prussian parvenu and all his like, when they looked down on the Latin culture, which was the deepest driving force of the Great War. It was this feeling, profound, instinctive, often unconscious, which filled those who insisted most strongly that the end was worth the heart-rending sacrifice by which the War was won. It was not merely British Imperialism, nor merely French nationalism, nor merely, if at all, Russian Pan-Slavism. It was something in every man who really felt like a citizen of civilization, reminding him from what language the very word "civic" had come.

That is the fourth theory of the Great War; and few were they that found it. But about those four theories, I would ask the reader to remark a rather curious fact. On any of the first three theories, the War was a failure even where it was a success. It was a defeat for the conquerors. It was a loss to the winners. It was a thing not followed by any of the results that might rationally be expected to follow it. If it was *all* concerned with British commerce and prosperity, finding their rival in Germany, one would expect that British commerce would have grown more prosperous when British arms had grown more predominant. One would expect a boom in British trade following the slump of her rival. In fact, as we know too well, if poor old England went into the War for wealth, she got precious little out of it. In the same way, though in a less degree, we can say that France got precious little out of it. It was more certain that Germany was weakened than that France was strengthened. We all know what Russia got out of it. She got defeat, collapse, anarchy and the anti-national experiment of the Communist Jews. So that in all these three cases, we have the extraordinary conception of a great power fighting somebody for something, winning, and not getting what it fought for. There is this to be said for the unpopular fourth explanation; that it is the only one of which the sequel makes any sense.

If it was Germany against Britain, Britain was almost as much weakened as Germany. If it was Prussia against France, France was almost as much foiled as Prussia. If it was Austria against Russia, Russia was as much ruined as Austria. But if it was something older and yet more central, lying to the south in the old centres of our civilization, then the consequences are not quite so inconsequent. If it was, as we in our tiny group maintained, in the last resort simply Rome shaking off the barbarians— then nobody can say that Rome is ruined along with the barbarians; for Rome is in visible resurrection.

That is the meaning of the *cheerfulness* of Italy, which is the great mystery of post-war Europe. Of all those who in that great trial emerged triumphant, the Italians alone had the air of triumphing. It was not merely Mussolini; it was not even merely Fascism; it existed before either had appeared. I myself was in Italy the year after the War, passing through like a tourist, but even a passing glance showed things seen in no other country of the Allies; for instance, pencil scribbles on the walls, popular and even illiterate, but always to the same effect, "Italia vittoriosa"—Italy the Victorious. They had suffered with the rest, as much from privation and more from anarchy. They were in a hopeless muddle, but they were in a hopeful mood. Though it is never possible to prove these impalpable things of psychology, I believe the explanation I have given is the right one. A certain sort of people felt that a certain load had been lifted off them. And the people were the people of the old civilization which for centuries had been mocked for its divisions and its decay; but of which the subconsciousness had never forgotten that it was once not only the master but the maker of the world. And the load was the load of the modern practical prestige of the North; the notion that Germany and the new countries were the only progressive and prosperous countries. Everybody thought the centre of the earth had shifted from Rome to Berlin; just as they once thought that it had shifted from Rome to Byzantium. But in both cases it was the New Capital that collapsed and the world returned to Rome.

But in the modern case it was not only the fall of the New City but the fall of the New Theory. It was the check to the whole modern conception in the matter of new cities; the conception that progress is always progressing to new places and beginning afresh with new names. It was the notion that New York must be better than York, that New England must be better than England, that New Orleans must always have better prospects than Orleans; that Nova Scotia must always be in culture and philosophy a hundred years ahead of Scotland of the Scots. It was the notion that civilization is nomadic; or (as the progressive prefers to put it) on the march. The theory had turned men's thoughts throughout the nineteenth century to new countries and colonies as the only possible starting-places for new movements. The theory is not true. The chief result of the Great War was to prove that it is not true. Like any other theory, it can show particular examples that are true. But it does not represent the present practical trend of the truth. What has really happened in the world since the War, if old progressives were not too blinded by old prejudice to see it, is the rewakening of old places and the return to old shrines. Warsaw is Warsaw once again; and Cracow is even older and therefore newer than Warsaw. Europe is full of early mediæval things; the old kingdom of Bohemia; the old isolation of Hungary; the old empire of the Serbs. And if we look in the newspapers to see what is really happening, even the newspapers can hardly disguise from us that there is once more conflict in Jerusalem and once more order in Rome.

Only the aged have a future. A wind of death is coming in which only the very old will not die. These are unfashionable and unfamiliar sentiments, in a time when a superficial hustle and heartiness about new codes, new countries and new colonies fills up so much of the newspapers to the exclusion of the news. But they are so true, in the light of history, that the mere advocates of novelty have to take refuge in prophecy. They are certainly true of the history of Rome, whose profound roots have taken hold of the earth when so many newer and lighter seeds have been blown away. Everything was done to remove Rome from Rome. The Emperor was taken away; but the Pope remained. The Pope was taken away; but the Pope returned. The former movement could not make a new Rome at Byzantium. The latter could not make a new Rome at Avignon. The former had behind it the great civilization of the Greeks; the latter had behind it the great civilization of the French. The Greek Emperors thought they could move it easily to the East, as the French Kings that they could move it easily to the West. But the New Empire and the New Nations had the disadvantage of youth; which in these things is to die young. Rome is a rock not easily moved; and in the course of but a few centuries, as history goes, she had seen the French Monarchy go down before the Jacobins, as she had seen the Greek Empire go down before the Moslems.

Three times therefore, even in the period covered here, there had passed over Rome in ruin a miracle that woke the dead. Rome had become materially a rather deserted diocese; but deserted, disdained and dominated, the diocese rose up and made a new Empire. Rome was even more deserted in the Avignon epoch; but revived. Again, fallen to be mere local princes, the Pontiffs yet dug up a lost world, and ancient Roman statues could again be made in Rome. And now, before our very eyes something of the same almost spectral revivification has lifted and transformed the dust; and modern madness and treason and anarchy have brought forth, not ancient Roman statues, but ancient Romans.

I know that the phrase is violent, and I use it because the transition has been violent. I know all that there is to be said against such violence and such a transition, and I shall state plainly in another place where I think it has really done evil and violated things that it would be better to preserve. At the moment I am only, as a common witness out of a crowd, bearing testimony to a miracle. I have seen men climbing the steep stones of the Capitol carrying the eagles and the *labellum* that were carried before Marius and Pompey, and it did not look like a fancy-dress ball. I have seen a forest of human hands lifted in a salute that is three thousand years older than all the military salutes of modern armies; and it seemed a natural gesture and not a masquerade. I have seen a great and glorious people, torn through ten centuries with too many splendid passions, suffering always from the division and distraction that comes from the very nobility of passions, now plainly possessed, solidly and visibly in the sunlight, by an ancient human passion forgotten for many centuries; the passion of order. It is not merely discipline, which is a thing taught and imposed; it is not the heavy regimentation which pedants in "scientific" states would impose on herds from which they stand apart; it is itself a popular appetite and a popular pleasure. It does not seem incongruous with the high republican memories of that steep road and that stony citadel; for the very faces of the crowd carrying the eagles or the Fasces are not the shifty obliterated faces of a modern mob, but those faces of the old Roman busts which we have tried in vain to trace or remember when we saw them in beggars in Naples or waiters in Soho. So far as a man may give the sense of his experience in a single phrase; he has seen the return of the Romans.

Unconscious symbols are sometimes more solemn and imposing than conscious ones. I have heard it said that the Fascists themselves had originally a rude popular symbol of their own, which was only afterwards identified with the Fasces of their fathers. I know not if this is true in fact; but it is true enough in fancy, in the strange way in which we can trace something impersonal and yet individual in the large unconscious patterns made by the movements of such a people. There is a sense in which the historian is impressed rather by the slowness than the swiftness of Rome. And while the eagles remain as the obvious emblems of its swiftness, there has always been something very moving to my own imagination in that vast communal animal the Tortoise, that was made by the interlocking of the roof of Roman shields; logical as the radiating sections of a mathematical diagram; vast like the labyrinthine plan of a primeval city; and moving slowly into battle, but not turning back. We may call that other creature, if we will, the type of the Roman slowness. But it was the Tortoise that won the race.

These rough impressions, these popular after-thoughts, have often something in them truer than the more self-conscious heraldry. They are not always filled with the obvious swagger of lions and eagles. For that matter, it might be fairly said in such a fancy that the Roman battering-ram was only a sort of bellicose sheep. And I can well believe that even the terrible Fasces, whether in their old or new evolution, were something as homely and accidental as what they really look like; the bundle of a wood-cutter. This quality of something close to the common earth is in all Italian history; as Cincinnatus came from the plough and Mussolini from the village forge.

I was coming out of the church of the Ara Cœli, where I had been hearing Mass, when the vanguard of the advancing column came climbing up the rock, almost as if they were storming an alien citadel rather than re-occupying their own. Right up against the statue of the Stoic Emperor they bore the very emblems that he knew; so that if ever those blind eyes could see, they might have opened to see again the Lictors and the immemorial initials of the Senate and the People of Rome. As I was in the first shock of beholding so strange a resurrection, I heard the high, thin but refined voice of an American lady saying in my ear, "Say (or words to that effect), is Mussolini here?" If she had asked whether Marcus Aurelius or Mark Antony was here, I should have felt it appropriate; for the moment I had forgotten Mussolini. It is something of an achievement to get oneself forgotten in that way.

I answered, rather abruptly but I trust politely, that I was told he had made a speech earlier, in the city, but had now left it; but I warned the young lady that I had no authority but rumour.

"Well," she said (and it were vain to deny, in spite of many disclaimers, that it sounded like "Wal" to me), "if he's here, I just want to see him; that's all."

And then, in that instant, I know not why, there suddenly blazed upon me the true meaning of that sort of American travel and curiosity. It is due to American truthfulness; or at least that truth which the Puritan conscience of New England still demands. I had always been puzzled about why all these good, healthy, innocent Americans bother so much about European travel at all. They come a thousand miles to look at things which they do not pretend to like or understand; shrines and relics and religious pictures only enjoyed from one angle of artistic taste. I remember a worthy Rotarian, who would come across the vast ocean to see the dim and dreaming city of Bruges; and positively insisted on visiting the Chapel of the Sacred Blood. He had had some difficulty in finding it; but he was not to be deterred. I heard him shouting across the crowded market-place to another Rotarian, "Say, here, where's this Blood they talk about?"

Now you would think a man of that sort had no possible motive to visit the chapel at all. If he had said the chapel was a mouldering sink of superstition, I should respect him. But I never could make out why people should so ardently desire what they so honestly despise; or why they should commit idolatry without the excuse of faith. And somehow, the American lady's words unexpectedly enlightened me. She was not thinking about Rome but about Boston or Byzantium, Pa., or wherever she lived. And her honourable New England conscience would not allow her to say that she had seen Mussolini, if she had not seen Mussolini. To have seen him as a mere dot in that huge crowd of heads would have been quite enough. She wanted to be able to say quite honestly to Sadie or Clytie when she got home, "I *did* see Mussolini."

It would have been quite useless if I had said to her: "What you see now is an astonishing historical resurrection. Those letters on that label on that spear are three thousand years old. The world no more expected to see them again than an ensign with ancient Egyptian hieroglyphics. That salute the men are making as they pass the Unknown Warrior's Grave, is something almost as remote as the stiff salutations in Assyrian sculptures. It may be all insolent and wicked, as God knows a great deal of that old world was insolent and wicked; but you have seen something in your travels, if you have seen such slaves and tyrants rise from the dead."

It would be no good to tell Sadie that she had seen a ghost or a return of the past. But though I have all too little of the American virtues in this matter, the verbal exactitude or the intellectual courage of the interviewer, I will confess to so much of sympathy with the lady that I did not wish to leave Rome without having seen the mysterious and much disputed person to whom so much of this change is due.

I went into the black cavernous entry of one of those great castles or palaces, some of them very ancient, which are still used for many of the public offices, and showed a sentinel an order I had received from headquarters, granting me an interview, as was formally stated, with the Foreign Secretary; or in other words with the present head of the Italian State. I passed from official to official, a little more rapidly than is my experience in such attendances; and was eventually shown into a large room which seemed to me like a vast wilderness of tessellated pavement. The only other two things of which I was conscious was a picture of a Venetian sort on the wall, a portrait of some departed prince or ruler I imagine, and a small table at the other end of the perspective from which an alert, square-shouldered man in black got up very rapidly and walked equally rapidly right across the room, till we met not far from the door. He shook hands and asked me in French if I minded talking in that language. I said I did it badly but would do my best. Then we sat down by the little table and had a conversation which remains in my mind as a sort of puzzle; for, to tell the truth, I do not quite know what happened or whether I was talking at random, or prompted by my companion, or, in short, how the conversation came to be what it was.

I am sorry to say that I have nothing to report about the great Fascist's views on Fascism. I have formed some opinions on it, as will be seen elsewhere, but they were mostly collected elsewhere; I formed certain impressions of him, but they were not necessarily connected with his office. Benito Mussolini has a face of the type to be found here and there in Italy; it is nicknamed Napoleonic, but the term, though partly true, rather misses the point. Its peculiarity is that, in spite of bulging brows and a prominent chin, there is everywhere else an effect of the face being concave; a hollow look in eyes and cheeks between the heavy brow and the heavy jaw. It might be called the reverse or mould of the comic face caricaturists give to noodles, with large prominent noses and retreating brows and chins. As a face, it fits very well into that mask of bronze which is so much paraded by

friends and enemies and called Mussolini. The mask of
bronze stands for something, like a crest; but I rather
fancy it is part of the fighting-armour, like a vizor. Anyhow, there is very little of that in the man's personal de-
meanour in private. There is a great deal more fun in him
than masks of bronze are supposed to indulge in; he
laughs readily and he is not an Italian for nothing. He has
the vivacity of gesture; and one or two movements that
may on public occasions have a touch of the theatrical,
such as the weird power that some actors possess, of making his eyes suddenly shift and shine. It may be natural
enough, but I should not complain if it was in a sense oratorical. I know that a dictator must be a demagogue for a
time; just as a demagogue must be a dictator for a time. I
know that militant and democratic Latins cannot be led
by the merely familiar and good-natured smile of the old
squire or the constitutional monarch. It was for none of
these reasons that the conversation was curious, and, had I
been merely poking for political secrets, disappointing.
The legend of the mask of bronze has left many people
with the impression that Mussolini has no topic except
Mussolini. The best comment upon this is to record that
the very first thing he did was to dump me down in a
chair and ask me about the Disestablishment of the
Church of England.

In short, to put it in one way, I did not interview him
because he interviewed me. He put a rapid succession of
questions covering a wide field, but mostly concerned

with my country and not his. Doubtless had I been a truly valuable and trustworthy journalist, of the sort that rises by merit in his profession and attracts the approval of the Wise and Good, otherwise the big newspaper owners, I should have been "quickest on the draw" and got my questions in first; and not been hindered (as I so often am) by a musty Victorian tradition of manners, leading me to allow my host a say in the trend of conversation. In two or three snappy seconds I should have been saying, "And to what do you attribute your success, Signor Mussolini?" and all those recognized openings, such as, "And what, Signor, was the proudest moment of your life?" And I might have gone down that smooth and slimy path to God knows what lengths, until I was asking, for the benefit of millions of readers, "Do you attribute your genius to your mother?" or, "Have you had throughout a continuous sense of the presence of God?" It is possible that he made me talk as an astute diversion to avoid these questions; anyhow they were avoided, first because I should in any case have avoided them myself, but also because he instantly started to ask me questions; questions on all sorts of things I should hardly have thought he had ever heard of; such as the debate on the Revised Prayer-Book. Something I said about Imperialism and Internationalism seemed to arrest his attention sharply and he said, "Ah, that is very interesting. Do you think it possible to give a different turn to the development of England?" I told him, in increas-

ingly halting French, that I knew it was difficult, or perhaps nearly impossible; but I did desire England to be
more self-supporting and less dependent on the ends of
the earth, for I thought such dependence had become very
perilous. Before I knew where I was, I found myself
talking at large about my own fad of Distributism; and
now, between my embarrassment and my excitement,
my French went all to pieces. God alone knows in what
language the last part of the conversation found expression on my side; or to what wild barbaric tongue, older
than Babel, its gasps and nasal noises might be supposed
to belong. Thinking it not improbable that Signor Mussolini might think I was mad, I rose as if to bow myself
out. He rose also and said, with what was probably irony
but was none the less most polished courtesy, "Well, I
will go and reflect on what you have told me." This
quality, I may remark, belongs to all Italians; to men of
much humbler station than Mussolini, though he also is
a man of the people. Wilkie Collins said somewhere that
the mark of a gentleman was "unsought self-possession,"
and Italians are a nation of gentlemen. A common plas-
terer or painter or something fell off a ladder, so to speak,
into our bedroom in the most embarrassing manner; but
he was not at all embarrassed. He apologized exactly as
an English duke would have done. And certainly there
is the very extreme of this unsought self-possession in
the blacksmith's son who now bears in Italy, in its old
and real sense, the name of the Duke.

[203]

As we parted, I said, "Vous me pardonnez, Excellence, que je parle français si mal," at which he laughed again and said, "Ah, vous parlez français comme je parle anglais."

And I went away, as I have already hinted, ruminating on something like a riddle. I hated the idea of having talked too much, instead of listening to a more interesting person; but I could not quite get it out of my mind that the interesting person had possibly intended that I should talk a great deal about my politics, rather than he talk about his. In any case, I apologize to everybody, and not least to Signor Mussolini; for this was a very irregular business and no example of an interview for The Young Journalist's Guide. But of one thing I am certain; that if the Dictator has used violence, it is not because he cannot use wit; and if he has narrowed his appeal to his own nation, it is not because he lacks an intelligent interest in the philosophy of the world.

I know it will be the general impression about this book that I cannot talk about anything without talking about everything. It is a risk that I must accept, because it is a method that I defend. If I am asked to say seriously and honestly what I think of a thing, such as the Vatican State or the Fascist Government, I must think about them and not merely stare at them. And there is no thinking of such things except in relation to the world in or against which they stand. A universal situation is the *cause* of Vaticanism or Fascism; and a local cause is certain to be false. In the first chapter, I found I could not explain certain statues to anybody, even myself, without insisting that they would not be there at all but for certain remote religious dogmas and distinctions. In this chapter, I realize that the first fact about Fascists is that there would be no Fascists, but for a vast and, as I think, ruinous landscape of the whole of Europe. The Roman statue stands up white against the dusty gold of the Greek Empire or the dark forest of barbarism; the Fascist stands black against all the faded party colours, all the rags and ribbons of a long political riot or carnival. I cannot say what I really think of these things, without such digressions; and I do not propose to say anything else.

When I went to Italy I had one dark suspicion in my mind, which prejudiced me against Mussolini and his government. It was not the statement that he was reactionary or militaristic, for I knew that such terms may mean anything and generally mean nothing. It was not the fact that journalism is not free in Italy; for, being a journalist myself, I am of course aware that it is not free in England. Naturally it was not, in my case, the fact that Mussolini has declined to act in the accepted and normal capacity of a Free Thinker; which is persecuting all those who choose to think that Catholicism is true. With much or most of all this or what it symbolized I roughly agreed; but there was something about which I profoundly doubted if I did not disagree. There was one little dark cloud on the horizon; one black speck of scepticism on the mind; which made me think that the whole business might have a meaning exactly opposite to everything that I meant.

This bit of bad news I had heard was that English travellers were now made much more comfortable. It was an indirect suggestion. I have forgotten how and where the horrid whisper first reached my ears; but it seemed as if some of my own country folk of the comfortable classes, travelling in the new Italy, had found that things went more smoothly for them. They were less bothered by thieves, which looked rather bad in itself. They were less troubled by beggars, which looked even worse. Thieves are theoretically things to be discouraged; though several saints, from St. Edward the Confessor to St. Francis of Assisi, were blamed for encouraging them. But beggars are manifestly sent by heaven to make the comfortable classes more uncomfortable and I must say that the beggars of Italy threw themselves into their task with an enthusiasm and success which may well have seemed somewhat excessive. Perhaps even comfortable people ought not to be made quite so uncomfortable as all that. And I can readily believe that some reform and modification may have been advisable and generally advantageous. But it is a bad thing in itself when foreigners begin to have it all their own way in any country; especially in a country of such great and generous traditions, and such Christian and kindly popular customs as Italy. It means that some popular patchwork, of little sacrifices and charities suitable to the people, is being torn across to suit some stupid external force that has money or push behind it. If ever I hear, in the course of the next ten years, that Americans are really happy in England, I shall know that the happiness of the English has departed.

I was rather reassured, however, on hearing that there were not so very many English people in Rome; and I was almost completely reassured when I found them, and heard them talking about the Fascist Government. I will say a word later, in a more serious sense, on how far I think that Government really has reacted towards regimentation too much; and whether a slightly larger infusion of beggars and thieves would not be a gracious indication of the growth of Christian fellowship. For the moment, it is only just to the present Italian Government to testify that it is by no means so much admired by foreign visitors as is supposed; and as I, in my first faint sickening dread, had fancied or feared. The English actually on the spot have many complaints to make of Mussolini; but it is not unfair to say that the most solid complaint is that he taxes them very heavily for living in his country. Every one would like to agree with his own countrymen in a foreign land; but I confess I do not quite see why Englishmen should have an indestructible natural right to live cheaply in Italy, if it is to the disadvantage of the Italians. Anyhow, it is sufficient to restore my confidence in Mussolini as a man who is acting, according to his lights, for the advantage of the Italians.

The fear I had felt that the old popular life of the South might have been nearly flattened out, to make a smooth highway for globe-trotters, has largely left me. I still think that Mussolini makes the old light-hearted Italian rather too responsible. But even that is better than being a common Member of Parliament; who perpetually says he is responsible, and never responds.

Before attempting, even in the vaguest way, a description of Fascism which may be mistaken for a defence of Fascism, I think it well to state that I doubt whether in the actual original Italian conflict I should have been for the Fascists. The party I should naturally have chosen is that called the Popular Party, which was specially the party of the Catholic Democrats. I have heard criticisms of it from reasonable critics; and I am exceedingly proud of the fact that the Catholic Democrats are chiefly criticized for having been too democratic. I remember especially the views of an Italian friend of mine, who is a moderate and critical supporter of Fascism, and who certainly would not dislike the Popular Party merely for being popular; or for sympathizing with the populace. He used the strong expression that the Popular Party was merely Bolshevism dressed in white instead of red; that is, Communism masquerading as Catholicism. It may be very perverse of me; but I heard this also with a deep feeling of pride; of pride in the party that I never had the chance to belong to. If the charge was false, it was only another of the endless contradictory charges with which Catholics are pelted whatever they may do; called slaves if they are loyal to a king, or rioters if they are compassionate to a multitude. If the charge was true, it was at least enough to refute and flatten out a good many other charges. When next we hear the Roman Catholic religion called the opium of the people, or charged with keeping the poorer classes in subjection by the hypnotism of superstition, we shall not forget that in the terrible hour of trial and division priests were blamed for going only too far in their denunciation of capitalism; and were blamable, if they were blamable, for yielding only too much to their indignation at the oppression of the poor. If this was indeed the excess by which the Popular Party failed, it was assuredly a most glorious and Christian failure; the sort of Christian failure which can generally in the long run be counted as a Christian triumph. For the time, it has failed; and many not without sympathy with it seem resigned, on arguable grounds, to its failure. But let it always be remembered that it was not put down by ecclesiastical authority, as so many would eagerly anticipate; it was put down by secular, scientific, highly modern and rational authority; not by the Church but specially and specifically by the State. The party led by a priest was too revolutionary for the party led by a Syndicalist. And in truth it does seem, for good or evil, to have been pretty revolutionary; and there were some things done in the course of strikes and agrarian actions which might surprise even my friend Conrad Noel, waving the Red Flag down at Thaxted. To this I will only add one hint, which I would not unduly emphasize, for I feel towards the memory of the Popular Party nothing but respect and regret. But my own private belief is that the real reason of its failure, in competing with Fascism which had many of the same ideals of social justice, was that it became suspect in the matter of the peril of patriotism. In one sense what is Catholic must be international; but it is never quite normal if it is not also national. When people try to thrust mere internationalism down the throat of Catholic nations, there is always a violent national reaction; so there was when English Socialists tried to do it during the Dublin Strike, so there will always be when cosmopolitan diplomacy tries to disarm the eternal vigilance of Poland. For Catholics know in their bones that men are citizens of a city, and not merely of a cosmos; and that the hearth is sacred as well as the altar. Anyhow, that is the only doubt I should myself have had about the original Catholic Popular Party; I should have had many more doubts about the Fascists; and I have a good many doubts still.

I am only concerned with Fascism here to the extent of suggesting that it is a revival, just as it is certainly a revolution. But I did not see the revolution; and in the nature of things I saw the merest segment of its result. I know too little about the facts to bear witness to them. I know too much about the modern newspapers to accept them as complete witnesses. It seems fairly certain that the revolution, like most revolutions, was stained by many infamous crimes and indefensible acts of violence; though they were not all on one side. But as I have passed much of my life in trying to persuade my fellow-countrymen that their fortunate immunity from the revolutions of the Continent is rather an accident for which to be thankful than a virtue of which to boast, I am bound to say the same of the Fascist Revolution as I have always said of the French Revolution or the Irish Revolution. I can hardly in honesty play the Pharisee over Mussolini when I refused to do it over Michael Collins; and it is just as easy, and in one sense quite as just to call Michael Collins a murderer as to call Mussolini a murderer. The fact is that they both did a number of things that nobody would think of defending except on the ultimate theory of national self-defence; that is, the theory that society was in dissolution and the fatherland at the point of death. That the readers of the *Morning Post* would denounce the Fenians and excuse the Fascists, while the readers of the *Daily News* would denounce the Fascists and excuse the Fenians, does not concern me. But since I have so often protested against this English self-righteousness about foreign violence, since I have so often suggested that Danton was not a gory baboon because he made the Terror or used the guillotine, that Irish rebels were not dirty assassins because they conducted a guerilla war, in the only way in which it can be conducted, against a much more powerful army—I do not propose

to treat the Fascists as fiends, merely because their rebellion was as nasty as rebellions always are.

All that concerns my argument is that there certainly
is a New Italy as there certainly is a New Ireland. I do
not approve of all the things that were done for the resurrection of Ireland; and I think it exceedingly improbable
that I should approve of all the things that were done for
the resurrection of Italy. But I have no personal information about the details of those things; the development of
my own thesis did not bring me in contact with them;
and as I cannot give a personal verdict of my own, I will
not repeat all the partisan verdicts of other people. And
though I have never thought it patriotic to encourage my
country in tyranny and stupidity, I should be a very poor
Englishman if I forgave the men who ambushed and
shot any number of loyal and innocent English soldiers,
and then reserved all my vindictiveness for the slayers in
a foreign fight, which I could not fully follow at the
time or fully study on the spot. The point here, as I say,
is that certain people saved Italy from something; or
sincerely believed that they were saving her from something. What that something was brings us to the only
question relevant here. And it is very relevant; for it is
something from which England has not yet been saved.

In short, I resent British superiority to foreign fury;
because it always assumes that the British have gained
placidly all that the foreigners would gain furiously. In
truth, it is not that English conditions are not so infuriat-

ing, but only that English people are not so infuriated. There is a great deal of good in their attitude; but there is good also in the other. And nobody can begin to understand Fascism, who does not know that it was not so much a revolt against the Communism prevailing in Russia as against the Constitutionalism prevailing in England.

It was even more than that. The first fact in favour of Fascism is one far more unfamiliar to its admirers than its opponents. In England at least, they are so ignorant of it that they do not even know they have not got it. They are so impotent even to imagine it, they could never even discover that it does not exist. Even to give it an intelligent name would probably only make it more unintelligible. If I were to say that the countrymen of Machiavelli had rediscovered The Prince, there would only be an impression that they or I were up to some trick or other. If I were to call it The King, I should be supposed to refer to the King of Italy, with the proper respect with which we refer to the King of England. But that would be about as true as translating Il Duce as The Duke. If I were to call it by the alternative name of The Republic, many would retain the strange idea that it is something to be got by removing the King. If I were to remind them that the word Republic was almost the same as the word Empire, and was used to the last as the true title for Empire, by the people who invented both words (and

[213]

both things) I should be pushed gently but firmly to the door; and possibly quite right too.

I will therefore abandon the attempt to talk in terms of reason or the history of political thought and say that there has come back in Italy a thing sometimes known in the ancient world, but very nearly unknown in the whole of the modern world. This thing is a Government, which is not merely a Governing Class. Above all, it is not merely an employing class. It is a third thing, distinct from employers and employed and corresponding to what was once called The Prince or the Republic. The Prince might be and often was a tyrant. The Republic might be and often was a tyranny. But it was not necessarily the same as the tyranny of the richest class in that state; it could on occasions tyrannize over that tyranny. There were states more on the modern model, where merchant princes ruled, not so much because they were princes as because they were merchants. Venice is the obvious example; but all the more obvious an example for being a rather isolated example. There were places where the merely wealthy not only ruled the state, but were the state. But as a general rule, before the age of modern finance and industry, the Prince or ruler was strong enough to be independent of the rich as well as the poor; and often made himself quite unpleasant to both of them. The King was not the nobles; he was not merely one of the nobles; he often cut off their heads or (what concerns the sociologist more) cut off their en-

tails. It has passed into a proverb that one of the royal
and romantic villains of history, like King John or Ivan
the Terrible, would treat great lords or abbots as traitors,
merely for being richer than he was. It is agreed that it
was a very wicked King who thus ruined the rich. It
would be a very good King who would do it now.

Now the main fact of modern times, as every one
knows, is that there has been a widespread quarrel between rich and poor; or (in the language of those rugged
men of the people who like the longest words they can
find in a dictionary) between capitalists and proletarians.
Now in most modern nations, especially those noted as
very modern nations, there are only these two contend-
ing things; there is no third thing that can attack them
both. There is a thing called a Government, of course, but
it is simply the capitalists or the servants of the capitalists. It is sometimes moderate and humane; because capitalists are sometimes moderate and humane. It is in various mild degrees sympathetic with Labour; because
some employers are in various degrees sympathetic
with Labour. Capital may be more or less consider-
ate when it controls Labour; but there is nothing
that can control Capital. In a big modern state like
America, for instance, it is ultimately Big Business that
controls the American government; because Big Business is bigger even than America. It is needless to add
that it is much bigger than England. The notion that
when some well-meaning noodle of a nobleman, or some

respectable hack of a lawyer, presides over a Capital *v.*
Labour committee, he is equidistant from the two points
of the two parties, is a fancy that will amuse any one acquainted with practical politics. He may, and generally
does, do his best; he may want to meet the workers half
way; but so may any one of the employers. But the work-
man who simply sees and says that another man with a
black coat has been added to his black-coated adversaries
is talking the only common sense of the case. There have
been occasions when independent gentlemen have really
tried to differ from the employers. In those cases they
have always failed to stop the employers. Modern government is capitalist government; not as a term of abuse,
but as a fact of science. As it is expressed in the beautiful
diction of the golden West, what the Big Man says
goes. But it does not go in Italy.

I do not mean that Italian government is my ideal of
justice, or that it does not ever support the employers, or
that it might not support them where I should oppose
them. I mean that it may support them; but it *can*
oppose them. The ordinary modern government cannot.
The ordinary regular respectable representative government, by Wall Street via Washington, cannot. The ordinary British government, by the Party Fund via the Parliamentary group, cannot. The new Italian government
can; and it has again and again adopted a policy quite
unparalleled in the whole political world of to-day; which
is worthy of a sharp and close attention which it has

hardly received. It is not Socialism; it is not Distributism; but it is distinguished and divided in a most startling manner from anything to which we are accustomed
as Capitalism. It is in fact simply Command; the national
law overriding the industrial law. Perhaps there is no
shorter way of putting it for English readers than to take
an English example. How would the Fascist method, for
instance, have applied to the last great Coal Lock-Out
(mysteriously described as a Coal Strike) which led to
the interlude called the General Strike?

It will be the more amusing, because anybody who remembers that business will remember that the Conserva-
tive Party rang with appeals for British Fascists—for very
British Fascists. The dear old ladies who search the
Morning Post for the secret of the Bolshevism of their
cooks and housemaids were sure that Mussolini was the
man to sustain them in that unequal encounter. The
jolly old soldiers whose conversation gives colour and
warmth to the meetings of the Putney Primrose League
were quite sure that these Fascist fellows were the sort
of fellows to deal with the striker fellows, who were
neither more nor less than Bolshevist fellows. All those
aunts of the human race, whom it has heartlessly left
stranded at Bath or Brighton, prayed aloud that Heaven
would send us, in the dreadful hour of the Coal Strike,
a real resolute Dictator like this man Mussolini. And indeed, I was tempted to join in their prayer. For all those
worthy Tories who wanted a Dictator like Mussolini

would have jumped out of their skins if they had got one. Nobody would have been more astounded by what Mussolini had to say. For, by every analogy from his own theory and practice, what he would very probably have said in the British Coal Crisis is this:

"You, Coal-owners, will continue to pay the Coal-miners the full wage which they demand; and if you do not, I will take it from you. If you say your business will be ruined, you must take the risk; and leave it to us and the future. If it is really ruined, in the sense of your being liable to appear in rags begging in front of the churches, we will do something for you out of Government funds. We will help you to do justice. We will bribe you to do justice. But we will not suffer you to do injustice. We will not suffer you to oppress the hireling in his wages; we will not suffer you to discharge the hireling without his wages, and add to the chaos of unemployment. We will not dispossess you as the employer; but you must go on employing. We will not argue about the abstract rights of your being the paymaster; but you must go on paying; and paying properly. See to it, therefore, that every man jack among the Miners receives the full payment which you say you cannot pay, when he turns up at the pay-desk on Saturday; and if you do not do it, *Corpo di Baccho,* you will get what is coming to you."

That is what Mussolini would probably have said to our Conservatives and Coal-owners. That is the economic expedient of Fascism. The policy is not especially my policy; the philosophy is not perhaps my philosophy. It is open also to a number of quite arguable objections. It may be said that the method is not in the narrow sense economic; that it is a policy of desperate patching up, like Inflation or the Dole and so many desperate remedies in our declining and perhaps dying industrial world. It may be said, what is but another aspect of the same thing, that it is not certain how long such a method could possibly go on; though a more prosperous Italy, attained thus in the meantime, might yet meet the question. It has the disadvantage, from my personal point of view, of accepting a little too automatically the assumption of the modern relations of employer and employed. It may be an interference with liberty; it is certainly an interference with property. It may be a makeshift materialistic *coup d'état* blind to the best ideals in individualism. But it is not being bossed by the big employers; and every British government has been.

That is the first note of Fascism; * and I do not recognize the wood-notes of the Primrose League or the pastoral pipe of Mr. Baldwin. It was because Mr. Baldwin would not talk thus firmly to employers that there is now a Labour majority in Parliament. It is because Mussolini does talk thus firmly to employers, whatever his

* I do not know, of course, what Mussolini thought of that particular case, or what he might do in identical cases. I merely point out what is *peculiar* to Fascism in bullying or bribing employers to employ. We need no Fascism to teach us to unemploy. We achieve that with the most constitutional ease and calm.

errors in other ways, that there is no Labour opposition to him worth talking about in the new Fascist State. I shall have plenty to say in a moment about what is really worth talking about, in the way of opposition and criticism in the Fascist State. There are some ways in which I think it has gone wrong; but I am not just now even trying to show where it has gone right. I am trying to show where it has gone; and along what rather new and unique path it has travelled. And the first fact to note about it is this despotic independence of the ordinary capitalist régime; which is well illustrated by its ordering businesses to pay big wages or punishing business men if they discharge workmen unjustly. For the moment I do not even argue that it is a good thing; I argue that it is a third thing; acting independently of Trade Magnates and Trade Unions and capable of giving orders to both. And I say of this what I said at the beginning; that it is, for good or evil, the return and re-establishment of government; of government as a separate thing distinct from the differences and interests of the governed. I can easily imagine objections to it; I could listen with patience to many current arguments against it. But I cannot listen with patience to the current arguments for it. I cannot tolerate the tosh of weak snobs and vulgar reactionaries who wail aloud for a Strong Government and never fancy for a moment that they might themselves feel its strength. I have no respect for the feverish and feminine aristocrats who are always

asking for a Master, and then imagine that he would be
their servant. People of that sort have never even imagined the meaning of the word Government; since they
cannot picture themselves as governed but only as governing. And there is no sharper way of bringing the
point home to them than by the test of the great dispute
of the Miners, about which their newspapers talked such
nonsense four years ago. For there is a simple answer to
their cry of what Mussolini would have done in the Coal
Crisis. There never would have been any Coal Crisis. The
Coal-owners would have been forbidden to make one.

I have always called myself a Liberal, though I preferred to call myself a Radical, because it is not so respectable. I would willingly call myself a Republican anywhere except in America; where that is disgustingly respectable too. But by the word Republican I should mean
something that has really very little to do with the presence or absence of a modern constitutional monarch. It
means what St. Thomas Aquinas meant when he said
that there was needed to make a city a mob of free men;
that a commonwealth consists of citizens equal in their
civic rights as symbols of their human dignity. This civic
ideal is not in all cases inconsistent with monarchy, but
it is, in my opinion, inconsistent with aristocracy. The
mob which is one thing may have a monarch who is
one man; he is not only the expression of its unity but
even of its equality. But it is, I think, a totally different
ideal that there should be two sorts of citizens; as for

[221]

instance, free men and slaves. And when I called myself a Liberal or Radical in English politics, I meant that I was opposed to the spirit of oligarchy in that society; to the big estates which prevented the existence of small proprietors; to the big employers who subordinated the interests of the employed; to the one large shop-keeper who swallowed many small shop-keepers, and so on. Whether many other Liberals, or any other Liberals, ever meant this by Liberalism I will not claim to say; in later days I have had my melancholy doubts. But I do say that such a war of democracy against oligarchy means something; or would mean something, if anybody would wage it. Only when we pass from the theory of Liberty to the facts of Liberalism, we find ourselves facing certain facts; and these are exactly the facts which the Liberals will not face.

The Republican movement, beginning at the end of the eighteenth century and continuing in the Radicals and Liberals of the nineteenth, was struck down by a deadly disease; and would not even consult a doctor. That is what is chiefly the matter with modern Representative Government; that it will not admit that there is anything the matter. It persistently refused the offers of comparatively sympathetic French Nationalists and Bonapartists, Irish Sinn Feiners and English Independents of various kinds, to take it away to a hospital; until the Italian Fascists, in a fury, locked it up in a lunatic asylum. The biggest and most outstanding events in European history are never recorded in newspapers, and hardly perhaps in official reports; and there is very little record in the Parliamentary debates of the great historical incident of the Decay of Parliament. But it has happened, exactly as the Great War and the French Revolution has happened; the only question that remains is whether by tracing the causes of the malady we may form some notion of the cure.

The Republican ideal fell, like most things, by suicide; by cutting its own throat or contradicting itself. But it did in a rather special and startling degree contradict itself. This is especially true in one matter which immensely concerns the Fascist reaction; and it can be put in two sentences. At the start The Republic simply meant The Public Thing. At the finish The Republic simply meant The Secret Society. It had become by far the least public of all possible forms of government. It had become a system in which membership of the public body that could be criticized was far less important than membership of a private body entirely protected from criticism; sometimes by a denial of its existence, always by a denial of its object. It is quite a mistake to suppose that this reversal of the Republican idea was a mere matter of words and forms. The first Republicans were perfectly sincere in wishing their rule to be as public as possible. The best men of the French Revolution really were men of the Forum and the market-place; men living as far as possible under the open sky; men like statues standing almost permanently in the street. An American like Jefferson seemed really to wish to live not only in a white house, but in a glass house; that he might receive the supreme presidential privilege of being pelted with stones. Doubtless this candour became a cant, like all good things; and it is now rather the fashion to make fun of it. But in this matter I am Jeffersonian; and prefer the old America to the new. I have much more respect for the old Publicity which meant that we should know all the worst that could be known about the rich and the rulers, as compared with the new Publicity which means that we are only to know all the best that the rich choose to say about themselves.

Anyhow, that was the Paradise of Publicity, as conceived by the first Republican idealists. And with the entrance of the Secret Society, which was the entrance of the Serpent, came the Fall. I know that some maintain, in the Manichæan manner that the Serpent had created the world, including the garden; or, in other words, that the Secret Society created all the democratic ideals from the first. I believe this to be nonsense, because it takes no note of the natural appeal of those ideals. I have always sympathized with those democratic visions; and I never belonged to any secret society. But however it may be in the squabble about dates and details, the broad truth is that thousands of people thought they were establishing a broad and open brotherhood of all men; but with remarkable rapidity the power passed to small and secret brotherhoods of conspirators. The part played by the Freemasons in the politics of every European country was a thing perfectly well known to every man in practical politics anywhere; but it was never discussed in Parliament; certainly it was never discussed by Parliamentarians as a danger to Parliamentarism. We need not discuss here all the various kinds of nonsense, on both sides, on the subject of the Freemasons. They were not Masons; they were certainly not Free; in their most important fields of action they were not even free to say that they were bound.

But there was another element in the old Republican ideal, thus so swiftly and strangely ruined. This was the fact that it did originally denounce Luxury as the great enemy of Liberty. It will provoke a roar of amusement, and amazement, among modern Parliamentarians, to inform them that there was quite a clear ideal of Poverty among the first and best Jacobins, as sincere in its way as that among the first Franciscans. The accepted proof of a politician's soundness was that he should be honourably poor; there was something in it of what we call the Simple Life and they call Republican Simplicity. Few realize that the name of Napoleon grew glorious, not only through his glory in the matter of victory, but because he had a good name in the matter of living simply and paying his way. I need not attempt to measure the huge and ghastly reversal of all that in modern politics; in which so many liberals have been so very liberal to themselves. Luxury has become almost another name for politics; there is no world where it is so insolently assumed that money must fly on the most flying pleasures. As the poet wrote:

The evil power which buttressed privilege
And went with women and champagne and bridge
Broke—and Democracy resumed her reign
Which went with bridge and women and champagne.

I am not Puritanical about these things; and I do not mind the pothouse politician nor grudge him his pot of beer. But I do remark that professional politics has got itself mixed up with a plutocratic orgy at the very opposite extreme from its original ideals. That excessive exorbitant ever-encroaching Luxury is the cause of three-quarters of the corruption that has rotted out the vitals of Parliamentary government. And when next we hear poor old Robespierre, or some rather priggish Republican, jeered at as a sentimental bore for saying that the Republic is founded on Virtue, and that it cannot endure without the simple and laborious worth of the Virtuous Man—let us look a little at the sequel and salute him; and admit that he was not so far wrong.

Now without pretending that Mussolini is an ideal Republican, without denying the sense in which I say he is a real Reactionary, I do think it rather interesting to note that he has reacted violently against those two modern Republican vices in the name of the two ancient Republican

virtues. He has reverted to the original ideal that public
life should be public; and emphasized it in the most
dramatic manner by stamping on the Secret Societies as
on a tangle of vipers. And he is quite as serious, I might
say quite as solemn, as Robespierre himself, on the subject of the civic necessity of Virtue. That is to say, for
those who do not know Latin or understand the Latin
use of words, he feels the same sense that social life de-
pends on that sort of stoical and virile morality, which
some call merely negative morality. Many a modern
young man on the make would probably laugh at him,
but Jefferson would have understood him perfectly.
Therefore it seems to me something more than a coincidence that the great Fascist has actually rescued the two
lost and neglected ideals of the ancient friends of freedom. Liberals of the nineteenth century tradition need
not necessarily agree with him; I shall be quite contented
if they are ashamed of themselves. I am quite ready to
join them, since I also have been one of them. We ought
never to have allowed irresponsible organizations, with
secret signs and pledges, to undermine the pure publicity
of the Republic. We ought never to have allowed irresponsible hoards and hauls and mushroom fortunes, with
all their trail of vulgarity and vice, to be mixed up with
those whom we chose as champions of democracy. Republicans should never tolerate a Secret Society. Republicans should never tolerate a Secret Fund. Radicals should
never have tolerated such a tangle as that of luxury, laxity

and secrecy; and they have themselves to thank if somebody has suddenly turned round and refused to tolerate them.

It is chiefly, however, the hypocrisy about Secret Societies that has ruined the Liberal cause throughout Europe. They are now, in some right or wrong fashion, being rooted out by Fascism. They ought to have been rooted out by Liberalism. They ought a thousand times to have been rooted out by Republicanism. They are, in every term of their very nature, a denial of the Republic. It is this secrecy, and the secrecy about the secrecy, the silence about the silence, that has, if not justified, at least produced, the rough and ready violence of the reaction. An armed minority attacking a mob of other minorities is not fairly playing the game of democracy. Granted; but a secret oath sworn against the public vote, and a private combination to betray all public combinations, is also not playing the game of democracy. It is not altogether surprising if, after about eighty years of that incessant betrayal, people have grown tired of the game. People have grown tired of it even in England; where they never played that particular game even hard enough to grow very tired. Hence, for instance, Freemasonry has in England a very harmless tone; for where men do not take any politics seriously, they naturally do not take even secret politics seriously. But they have only to cross to Ireland to find all the Lodges are Orange Lodges and as Anti-Catholic as the Grand Orient. But what would most

Englishmen feel about the mere facts of foreign politics; if they were ever allowed to hear of them? To mention only one fact; suppose it were discovered that the Rationalist Press Association could prevent any young English officer from getting his company or his regiment, in the due course of promotion, if it could be shown that he went to morning service at his parish church at eleven o'clock. Suppose there was no promotion whatever for anybody except agnostic captains or atheist colonels; and documents existed in the War Office with black marks against any soldier who went to any service. That would be an exact description of the official documents about the French Army found under the Freemason Government. If that is Democracy, I am amused. If that is Liberty, I am still more entertained. If that is Liberalism, to which I suppose myself to belong, I am considerably concerned.

I conclude therefore, upon this point, that it is not so much that Fascism offers no points upon which it should be attacked, as that Liberalism has unfortunately lost the right to attack it. But it is not so much that Liberalism might under better conditions have really attacked Fascism. It is that Liberalism under any conditions ought to have attacked corruption and conspiracy and above all plutocracy; and, for all practical purposes, it never did. If the original Republican and civic ideal had been true to itself, there would never have been any need for a Fascist reaction against it; or the setting up of Dictatorship as an alternative to Democracy. I, for one, should have infinitely preferred that the purgation of our plutocratic politics should have been achieved by Radicals and Republicans. It was they who did not prefer it.

The soul does not die by sin but by impenitence. Human institutions also, which are all made in the image of the human soul, perish not because they have sinned but because they have not repented. It is an old story in the case of the old tyrannies; as when men said that the Bourbons had learnt nothing and forgotten nothing. The same process by which the ideals of the French Revolution overwhelmed the French Monarchy has in turn overwhelmed the ideals of the French Revolution. But it was not because the politicians were unpardonable; but because they would not even ask for permission, let alone for pardon. It was not because they were always as black as they were painted; but because they were never as white as they were whitewashed; and they were always whitewashed. What is the matter with Parliamentarism is that it says there is nothing the matter with Parliamentarism. That is the attitude which in every case of every institution has always produced some sort of riot; and in Italy of the twentieth century the rioters have become the rulers.

If, when all is said, I regret that Mussolini is a Reactionary, a thousand people will agree with me; and I shall entirely disagree with them. What they mean by a Reactionary is either something that Mussolini most certainly is not; or else something that I most heartily applaud him for being. For the first, those who imagine he is what we call a Tory have the total reverse of the truth; especially when they themselves are Tories. Mussolini is not half so much of a Tory as I am; he is not half so much of a reactionary as I might wish him to be. He seems to me to believe rather too much in new things and new methods, in science, machinery and modern experiment. On the other hand, in the sense in which he is, not indeed a Tory but subconsciously a traditionalist, I think he is a thousand times right. If it is reactionary to believe that human dignity is better than a sort of humanitarian impudence, that citizens who will not defend the city are not worthy to govern it, that women should be respected like mothers and not merely let loose to climb everywhere like monkeys, that piety and the honour due to the dead should be, as it was for the Pagans, a permanent religion for the living—if that is being a reactionary, I am a reactionary and I am very glad that he is a Reactionary. But, all the same, I am not glad that he is a Reactionary; and I think that being so much of a Reactionary is his one great mistake.

It all comes from the unfortunate habit of using words in their right sense. When I say reaction, I do not mean romance or tradition or loyalty or love of order, or any of these things even in their excess. I do not mean superstition or oppression or tyranny or slavery, or any of these things even in their milder forms. When I say reaction I mean reaction; the mere fact of reacting against something, or permitting that something to make us do something against it. It is said that in physics action and reaction are equal and opposite. It is a very good reason for keeping physics out of morals and metaphysics. The whole object of a wise man is not to react exactly as his opponents act; not to go so far in the one direction as the other man has gone in the other. He may, perhaps, after due reflection, go even farther; but he will not go exactly as far; nor will he go because the other has gone. He will not have his own movement made by another. If he does, though he ascend into heaven, it is only on one end of a seesaw, though he be swung like a club, he is only swinging like a pendulum.

A Reactionary is one in whom weariness itself has become a form of energy. He is one in whom even boredom boils and ferments at last by its own stagnation; and he acts not only with impatience but with the accumulated power of patience. He often acts very rightly; but it is his temptation to think that anything that was conventionally right is necessarily wrong. He deals too much in associations and too little in distinctions. He sees too much in social symbols; like the nineteenth century rebels who wore trousers because old-fashioned people wore knee-breeches; and then wore knee-breeches because old-fashioned people wore trousers. He tends too much to class all the features of an epoch together, and to date them rather than define them. And even when he is right, there is always a danger that what was really good in the previous society may be destroyed by what is good in the new one. I think it really true that Mussolini is reacting too much against the Liberalism of the nineteenth century. I do not refer especially to the violent language which the Duce, like every dictator, sometimes uses in a militant speech to a mob. That is a part of something that the northern temperament will perhaps never understand; the familiarity with fierce and even coarse expressions in the direct appeal of a true dictator to a true crowd. When Mussolini said, or is reported as having said, "I will set my foot upon the rotten limbs of the Goddess of Liberty," he was talking like Danton, who said of the royal execution, "France flings among the kings of Europe the head of a king." There are many refined persons in the North to whom that way of talking has never seemed to be quite nice. We are not democratic enough to have a dictator. But there is, apart from the diction, the materials of a distinction. What was wrong with the eighteenth century was not that a Monarchy was functioning, but rather that it was not functioning. What was wrong with the nineteenth century was not that Liberty was pampered or exaggerated, but that Liberty was pursued without being found. What was wrong was not Liberty, or even Liberalism; it was Liberals who were not even true to Liberalism, let alone Liberty. If the limbs of Liberty are rotting in the modern world, it is rather from lack of exercise than from having been worked to death. But I quite admit that as a catch-word, for what these modern people call an Ideal, it had been horribly worked to death; and the Italian orator was really expressing a very sensible contempt for a catch-word. But I think he is rather too prone to confound the vice with the virtue to which its hypocrisy does homage. Because a mean little minority, mostly members of a morbid secret society, manages to parade at many modern elections as The Majority, he is rather prone to deny any real rights to the real majority. But that is not to be superior to the professional liars of the political group, but rather to accept them at their own valuation. It is almost to be defeated; for it is to be deceived. Ours has not been an age of popular self-government; but of very unpopular secret government. It will be time enough to react against popular government when it has begun to act. We may begin to cry out for a Reactionary to make the world unsafe for democracy, when there has really begun to be any democracy in the world. Meanwhile I think it is an error to mix the ideal with the imitation and corruption; or to try to trample on an invisible goddess because a handful of dirty little politicians have lied when they called themselves Liberals. And it is perhaps especially an error for a man merely to repudiate the ideal of popular rule, when he has gone a great deal nearer than most modern rulers to making his rule popular.

That is what I mean by using the word Reaction or regretting that the Fascist leader is too Reactionary. That

[234]

he is not Reactionary in the snobbish sense of the current economic war, I have already shown. He is still a Syndicalist; and any number of our friends and neighbours would call him a Socialist. For though the word Socialist may be made to mean many things, its meaning among its most ordinary critics is simply that of a man who is ready to interfere in any way with those who have a lot of money. In that sense Mussolini would appear as dangerous as Trotsky to many in England who worship the one and execrate the other. Nor, as I have said, is he what some call Reactionary about the machinery of modern life; but rather breathlessly progressive. But if I may thus dare to use the word reaction as if it meant what it says, I think there is a case for saying that this revolution is too much of a reaction. I mean it in the psychological sense of a recoil; that he does sometimes recoil so much from anarchy as to talk only of authority; that he does so recoil from mere pacifism as to seem to endorse mere militarism; that he does recoil so much from the babel of tongues talking different heresies and contrary forms of nonsense, as to make his own moral thesis a little too much on one note. But this rigid insistence on the recoil is connected with another fact that must be understood.

I am not merely suggesting that the Blackshirt is not so black as he is painted. I am suggesting the more subtle truth that he paints himself more black than he is. It is a part of this reaction of disgust and disdain that it does sometimes disdain to appear even as popular as it may really be. A Parliamentary politician, whose name will bring a burst of jeers in any club or pub in all England, will talk as if he were followed night and day by the loving prayers and wafted kisses of the whole population. A Fascist leader, whose portrait is in every cottage, will sometimes talk as if he stood alone and at bay, with his back to the wall, facing the whole mob of Italy. It is, if you will, a case of variety in vanity; but on the whole I prefer the latter, possibly because I have seen so much of the former. The point may be put in many ways. We may say that the successful demagogue must denounce demagogy. We may say that the tyrant must despise popularity in order to be popular. The real question is that of the effect on freedom. Now we all agree about freedom. We all agree that we must not take liberty, except from people who take liberties. Unfortunately, it is those systems, which boast of not taking liberty, that do take liberties.

When a gentleman informs you that he is going to trample on Liberty with his boots, you might naturally expect that there would be unlimited trampling in practice, for it to be so frankly avowed even in principle. But, putting aside for the moment the matter of political journalism (to which I shall return later) I am by no means sure that the poor old goddess of Liberty has been trampled only here. She has been trampled a good deal, poor lady, all over the modern world. But in an ordinary everyday sense, she is a good deal more trampled in London than she is in Rome. The ordinary Roman citizen is not conscious of that network of nonsensical regulations and restrictions, about drinking and eating and buying and selling, which have become a common byword in our own comic papers. Some of the statements made about the Fascist regimentation in the foreign press I can tell, by experience, to be exaggerations. I was told in England that everybody in Italy was forced to walk in a certain way along the streets, turning to the left like an army on parade, and that people were perpetually arrested for the least deflection from the line. This is the wildest sort of overstatement. There are only three streets in Rome where it is necessary to walk on one side when going in one direction, and on the other for the other direction; and anybody who looks at the streets will agree that there is a good deal to be said for the general convenience of the arrangement. But an ordinary man stepping out of an ordinary house or hotel walks about exactly as he would anywhere else. This is a small matter; only it is in fact much smaller than the foreign critics suppose. To take a larger matter: Prohibition would seem insane slavery in Rome. But it is time we passed to larger matters still.

Mussolini does openly what enlightened, liberal and democratic governments do secretly. This is not the same as saying that Mussolini necessarily does right. Far from it; quite otherwise; heaven forbid. What enlightened, liberal and democratic governments do is generally wrong. What Mussolini does is, in my opinion, sometimes wrong, and I think there is more in the theory of the liberal democracies than could be inferred from his action—or theirs. But the point to grasp is that he does and defends what they do and do not defend. They conceal; they effect the same thing, because they think it convenient; but they do not defend it, because they think it indefensible. He is acting with his own principles of Fascism; they are acting against their principles of Freedom.

It will be the simplest test to take the two chief facts which the enemies of Fascism allege and which the friends of Fascism do not deny; but indeed rather proudly proclaim. Now whether or no these two limitations ought to exist in Italy, there is not the shadow of a doubt that they do also exist in England. The first is the fact that the Press is more or less varied in the subjects it discusses; but it is not free to say what it likes. And the second is that the voters at a political election have a limited choice, but not an unlimited choice. In a slowly and subtly modified aristocratic state like England these objects are attained by various ingenious methods of which I may say a word in a moment; in the democratic atmosphere of the Latins they have to be attained by very plain proclamation and direct action. But whatever action, or even accident, may have achieved the result, in both countries it is achieved. The British newspapers do in fact belong to two or three men, who have only to agree to suppress something and it is suppressed. The British elector does in fact have to choose between two or three candidates, each provided by a recognized Party Caucus and each supported by an unrecognized Party Fund. If anybody fancies that in modern England anybody can in fact start a really independent daily paper or stand as a really independent candidate, with the least chance of doing anything, let him try.

There do exist in fact in modern commercial states certain customs and practices which prevent, and are meant to prevent, free and frank criticism of those in power. One of the most powerful, for instance, is the interpretation of the libel law; which has this enormously practical custom added to it; that the wealthier the man or firm supposed to be slandered, the heavier are the damages imposed. This means, quite simply, in practice, that any poor man will certainly be ruined if he thus collides with any rich man. There are still perhaps honest Britons who will say that justice will always be done in British courts. I have no doubt that many Fascists would say the same of Fascist courts. But as it is quite certain that Bolshevists would say the same of Bolshevist courts, as also Spanish Inquisitors of the Spanish Inquisition, the test is somewhat uncertain as a guide to truth. And as I personally prefer to live in a world of reality, it is enough for me that I have never known one single case of any misconduct being brought home to a really powerful plutocrat in a court, though it were a fact that would be perfectly familiar and universally admitted in a club. It occasionally happens that adventurers already on the rocks, and known to have practically lost their money, do also legally lose their status or freedom; like Hatry or Hooley or Bottomley. But solid Capitalists, such as control the State, are not in fact convicted or punished in the courts of the State. In the United States they cannot even be punished for murder, except by terminable imprisonment often followed by tolerated escape. Let us frankly admit, therefore, that there is a terrible contrast between the tyranny which Fascists exhibit and the liberty which we are supposed to exhibit. But, as a fact, the best that can be said for our tyranny is that it is not so much exhibited.

I do not say that the Fascist has found the solution to the problem of modern liberty; but I do say that the modern Liberal has not even found the problem. Yet at present it is a very practical problem, and not one for wicked foreigners only. We all agree, as a platitude at the base of politics, that if there were no law or government at all, the brutal would trample on the weak and the result be not even an equal anarchy but an unequal oppression. What we do not see is that the same is now in fact true of the intellectual world, especially under our economic conditions. Merely to allow anybody to say anything does not in fact mean that everybody says everything. It does not mean, as the silly old Tories were

terrified to think it would mean, that a mob can roar
with a million voices. It means that a man who can buy
a megaphone can drown everybody else's voice. Merely
to allow anybody to print anything does not mean that
we shall all get our exquisite poems, our important private memoirs, or our grossly neglected pamphlets or pro-
grammes printed. It only means that any man with
money can instantly cover all the hoardings with his own
posters and leave not even a corner for our posters. Merely
to say that everybody can start a newspaper means in
practice that nobody can start a newspaper; except the
two or three people who can afford to start something
which for some time will not even pay. What we used to
call equality of opportunity really means unfair grabbing of opportunities; and grabbing by greedy people
from honest people and rich people from poor. Everybody
began by seeing this in the matter of material anarchy or
government by a free fight. They soon saw that, before
long, a free fight is not even free. Within our own time
they saw that it applied also to a ruthless economic struggle or competition; the sort of free fight that was
described as free trade. Nobody nowadays, however little
he may like the extreme called Socialism, supposes that
such a free fight is really a fair fight. But we have not
yet realized, what the Fascist in some rude fashion has
realized, that the same is to some extent true of truth
and error in their fight in the market-place; subject to the
lords of the mart. But it is even more so when we throw

[241]

into the scale, as we do in England, the capricious and plutocratic prosecutions for libel.

The whole case against modern Parliaments is the case about Corruption. There may be all sorts of different shades of opinion on that charge; but that is the charge. Some may be so happily at home in the modern world as to think that Corruption does not matter. Some may be so fantastically remote from the modern world as even to think that Corruption does not exist. But the charge now openly made against Parliamentarism everywhere is that it does exist. Now it is staringly self-evident, on the face of it, that nobody can debate that particular political problem at all, if he is restrained from making moral charges against public men, as if they were wanton little private slanders against private men. To say we are free to discuss politics, but must not accuse politicians of corruption, is exactly like saying that we are free to discuss Fascism but must not accuse Fascists of tyranny. That is to say, we must not accuse them of what they are accused of. We must not accuse them of the only thing which the world in general really thinks they stand accused. The Fascists do say this and avow it and act consistently upon it; but I am not necessarily here agreeing with them, or commending anything in them except their candour. But when once we have realized what the whole modern movement in the matter of Parliaments is, the proposal that we should politely talk "politics" and leave out "personalities," is simply ludicrous nonsense on the face of it.

It is quite simply refusing to discuss the modern problem of Parliamentarism at all. We can no doubt rave in leading articles about the inconsistency or illogicality or incompetence of politicians; but politicians are not now being criticized for inconsistency or illogicality or incompetence. They are being criticized for money-grubbing; they are being criticized for it everywhere in private life; if they cannot be criticized for it in public life, every intelligent critic is muzzled, exactly as if he were muzzled by Mussolini.

It is the same, of course, with the selection of candidates for Parliament; and especially of members of Parliament. The Fascists limit the choice and say so; we limit the choice and do not say so. We limit the choice by certain elaborate and carefully constructed methods of electioneering, which are practised with professional skill and success, like the method for neutralizing the negro vote in the Southern States of America. The most obvious method is making elections enormously expensive, allowing, encouraging or even insisting on expenditure on a complicated conventional etiquette of cars, canvassing, literature and the rest; so that the ordinary citizen could not conceivably compete with his ordinary resources. This at one blow limits all candidatures to capitalists of great substance, or to those to whom such capitalists wish to pay money through the instrument of Party Funds and subscriptions. Any such poor candidate therefore passes through a secret test exactly like the test of the Fascists;

except that it is a great deal more secret. The people who can pass this test of general approval by the plutocracy that rules our politics are not all people exactly alike; they are not automatic machines; they are not in all matters slaves. Nor are the people who can agree to give a general support to the Fascist régime. But in both cases the powers have a power of selection; and especially a power of suppression. The notion that the ordinary English voter lets his eye roll freely over all the crowds of his fellow citizens in the street, and then thinks he would like to vote for a nice looking navvy or a dear old pedlar, and does so, is far more of a wild fairy-tale than it would be to call the régime of Fascism a régime of unrestricted freedom. The average voter sees two men in top-hats, distinguished only by rosettes of different colours, two men he never saw before and never bothers about again; selected by somebody else for some reason unknown and often unmentionable; and between these, like a poor enslaved Italian, he makes his free and fearless choice.

I am well aware that two black shirts do not make a white. But I assure the reader that I am not, in this case, in the least trying to prove that black is white. I wish there were in the world a real white flag of freedom, that I could follow independently of the red flag of Communist or the black flag of Fascist regimentation. By every instinct of my being, by every tradition of my blood, I should prefer English liberty to Latin discipline. But there is the Latin discipline; and where is the English liberty? Not, I deeply regret to explain, anywhere in England. It is not a simple matter, in that connection, of the Italian wearing a black shirt and the Englishman a white shirt. If the Englishman wears anything, it must be a white sheet. It must be a garment of penance and lamentation, in honour of the great and glorious liberty—that he has lost. For he has lost it more completely than these men who actually boast of throwing it away. The general atmosphere of our Parliamentary politics is thick with proposals, such as Prohibition for instance, which the fiercest Fascist in all Italy would regard as absolutely demented interferences with private liberty and private life. If Mussolini were to propose Prohibition for Italy, everybody would think that he was quite literally a lunatic; they would realize it with tragic regret, as one would realize the physical madness of Swift or Maupassant or any other great man. Yet that is the sort of notion that comes quite naturally to the sort of country that is called a democracy, and is always in fact a plutocracy. I am not discussing such pharisaical persecutions here; but I do draw the line somewhere, for the honour of the English sense of humour. I will not listen to people who are first pharisaic about English drink and then pharisaic about Italian discipline. I will not hold up my hands in pious horror at the bullying ways of foreigners and then go back and bully my own poorer fellow-countrymen much more.

In a word; it is idle in our modern circumstances to

murmur that Fascist Italy is not free to say this word or that, as if others were in the habit of handling all words freely and putting all truths into words. Fascist Italy is founded on having gained the new and dreadful freedom to say one word; the one word that all the world had been forbidden to say. It claims, for good or evil, not to mention this or that, but to shout and cry aloud something that has been sealed up and silenced; the secret of our whole political system. That word was sealed up; and that word is loosened; and the men who heard it loud as a thunderclap are not for the moment thinking about liberty in lesser things. That word is Treason; which is the final and filthy flower of Corruption; the fact that men in high places, trusted with great popular responsibilities, could betray. They could, and they did, sell the just demands and defence of their own people to foreigners and invaders, covering it with a cosmopolitan cant, and acting under a cosmopolitan compulsion. That is what we are forbidden to say, in the countries of the capitalist newspapers; and that is what the Italians have gained the right to say under Mussolini's censorship of the Press. It is so vitally distinct from anything else that anybody else was allowed to say, that it may be a little time before they even want to say other things. When they do, I think it highly probable that a somewhat freer system will be advisable and will probably be established. The question is one of proportion and not perfection; and I am not in any sense offering this patriotic captaincy, born in the hour of peril, as a perfect thing. No; I should not specially describe modern Italians as men who are free. But I should describe them as men who are freed; freed from the special servitude and silence of our time; and above all, the servitude and silence which England still endures.

There is a logical case against Fascism; though it is seldom stated logically. Least of all, of course, is it stated logically in England. Considering how little the Anti-Fascists understand the Anti-Fascist case, it is hardly surprising if they do not understand the Fascist case. The intellectual criticism of Fascism is really this; that it appeals to an appetite for authority, without very clearly giving the authority for the appetite. It is valuable to know that something in our nature does cry out for order, especially after a real experience of disorder. But when we come to decide the nature of the order, there is, in fact, something disorderly about the way of deciding it. When I try to put the case for it in philosophical terms, there is some doubt about the ultimates of the philosophy. A very acute Italian friend of mine said that he was on the whole in favour of Fascism, but that he did not believe the current story that the country had been in danger of Communism. "Italians would never be Bolshevists," he said, "for Bolshevism you must have a general idea; and people here have only practical ideas." Perhaps in that very comparison there looked forth again for an instant the old antithesis of the Greek and the Roman; as when

the Greek iconoclast looked at the Roman image-maker.
I think it is possible that Fascism is too practical; possibly
too practical to last. Anyhow, it is curious that when I
cast about for a clear definition of the theory, I recall
first the words, not of a Fascist but a French Royalist. M.
Charles Maurras, a profound and subtle writer, wrote on
the first Fascist outbreak something like this, describing
democracy in general. "The mass of mankind is null or
toneless (*atone*) but the vigorous, intelligent and public-
spirited part of any particular people is not null or toneless." This is the idea implied in many remarks of Mussolini about the mistake of ruling by the Majority; and
the superiority of an intense and intelligent minority.
Any one can see the practical sense of this; as a matter
of practical politics; or rather of the present unpractical
politics. Every sane man knows the contemporary case
against the Majority merely in the sense of the Machine;
the mere mechanical register of electioneering. But there
is an answer to it; and I do not think that Mussolini, or
even Maurras, has considered it enough.

The answer is this; that after all there is only one majority; and there are a great many minorities. And, by a
curious coincidence, they are all intelligent, vigorous and
virtuous minorities; they say so themselves. What is the
exact nature of the authority which selects one sect of
authoritarians? The Majority may be a clumsy and cor-
ruptible test; but it is a test. The Majority test is like the
Monarchy test; it may produce poor specimens, but it

does not produce doubt or disorder about those produced. If the Czar's son is the Czar, there is always an unquestioned Czar; and if the man with most votes is the President, there is always an unquestioned President. But things may be a little more alarming if one vigorous minority meets another vigorous minority, and they set out to prove which is the more vigorous. If you say that somewhere or other in the state there is a spirited section, which has got to show its spirit, it will probably do it by conflict that is very spirited indeed. But setting seven sects to fight for authority will end in the very anarchy which you call on authority to end. This moral fact is only for a time masked by the material fact that one section is sufficiently strong and popular to silence the rest. In this sense Fascism may silence rebels in practice, but it invites rebels in principle. It invites any minority to claim the same superiority to Fascism which Fascism claimed to Communism. The common complaint against the Blackshirts is that they exercise too much authority; the real complaint against them is that they have too little. The Anti-Fascist argument is a Fascist argument. To believe in majorities as such is at least to let the majority rule; to believe in minorities as such is to call on all the minorities to rebel. That this is the last thing which the present "practical" Italians propose does not alter the ultimate difficulty of the doctrine underlying the law. I am far from being merely opposed to Fascism; but we must realize the perfectly reasonable sense in

[249]

which it may be said that the two really fixed and orderly constitutions are the old legitimist hereditary kingship and Majority Rule. Merely counting heads may be, and generally is, a silly business. But if we substitute valuing heads for counting heads, it is rather likely to end in cracking heads. The representatives of both vigorous and virtuous minorities will value each other's heads by butting each other like rams.

Thus Fascism is really forced by its own logic, or illogicality (as we happen to think it), up against the primary problem of a fixed moral philosophy. It is not enough to be a minority, when the Flat-Earthers and the Holy Rollers are a minority. There must be some test of truth, that can distinguish the sane from the mad minority. There must be an accepted ethical scheme; as there really was in the minds of the wisest men who founded the democratic experiment in the eighteenth century. Jefferson did not say that anything a majority did was right; he said that any violation of certain God-given human rights was wrong. Supposing, for the sake of argument, that we have now to deal with minorities and not majorities, it becomes even more essential that a minority should be tested by a morality. I do not altogether accept the Fascist view in these things; but the point is that the Fascist cannot really accept his own view, with any satisfaction to his own intelligence, until he has settled this question of permanent values. In short, Fascism has brought order into the State; but this will not be lasting, unless it has brought back order into the Mind.

I will not ask here, or perhaps answer adequately anywhere, the next great question of where this fruit of the true knowledge grows wild; or on the shores of what ocean, as the French writer said, the gods have rolled the stone that covers the truth of things. I can do no more than hint, in any work of this kind, how a free man is to find that staff and standard of justice that will support him against the spiritual pride of minorities as well as the automatic tyranny of majorities; that pearl of great price, the truth that is intrinsically true. I can only point out here that the logic of this revolution and reaction does bring it face to face at last with the need for some such reality; for an authority that is more than an anarchy that can manage to rule. As to where that strange growth is to be gathered, I can only answer that for me the crossing of the Tiber was like the crossing of the Styx; and that I sought it in a strange land.

VI · THE HOLY ISLAND

When I first saw one of the Papal Guard, or, to be exact, one of the Swiss Guard, I thought he looked like a harlequin. Many, I fear, will imagine that I mean by this that he looked silly or undignified. So little, I realize with a groan, after an obscure and laborious life of writing, does anybody know about anything that I think or feel. When I say he looked like a harlequin, I mean that he looked almost as sublime and splendid and poetical as a harlequin. But the comparison has several aspects, which throw a certain light on the understanding of Rome; and especially on the misunderstanding of Rome. To begin with, it is possible that some do not know that Harlequin was an Italian; just as there are some who do not know that Punch is Punchinello. But there is more than that in the international change. That which we in England used to call the Harlequinade was really the extinction of Harlequin. The English, with their glorious gift of a sort of gluttonous buffoonery, the sort of broad farce which made Chaucer's Miller and afterwards Mr. Pickwick and his convivial club, soon turned the fantastic figures of the Italian stage into sturdy and even stodgy clowns. Indeed they added the splendid name of Clown; for Clown is quite a different person from Pierrot. The English saturnalia consisted almost entirely of Clown and Pantaloon; always including the Policeman, who, being a responsible public official, existed for the solid social purpose of being made into sausages. The atmosphere of the original Harlequinade was quite different, and chiefly different in this; that the Harlequinade had something to do with the Harlequin.

In the old English version, which some of us are old and lucky enough to remember, the glittering figure with the rainbow raiment and the wooden but magic sword had already dwindled into a sort of dazzling interlude or parenthesis, twining and twirling his way with an equally objectless Columbine through the maze of the English clowning. But, as originally conceived, the proportions of the pantomime were quite different. Harlequin really was the hero; I might say even the serious hero. His sword was a sword, as well as a magic wand; and his motley was the masquerade of something mysterious and romantic, like a king disguised. Innumerable romances, of that half sentimental and half ironic sort, have been played out upon Italian stages with this group of old Italian puppets; and the coincidence is even closer when we turn from the scene to the scenery. Victorian England grew used to seeing the farce played out before a butcher's shop or a baker's shop or all the flat comicalities of a cockney street; and very glorious the farce was and I wish there were more like it. In the old Continental tradition of Pierrot and Harlequin the background was as different as the atmosphere; and if we ask what it was, we can really give no better answer than that it resembled very much the ordinary background of Rome. Its gardens were Italian gardens, its villas Italian villas; we might say that its very moon was an Italian moon. Indeed it is true to say that the back-scene of such an ancient comedy was really very like the landscape against which I saw standing the strange figure of the Papal Guard, with his striped and vivid raiment and his halberd of extravagant outline; a landscape of urns and broken pillars and the dark green growths of the South; and the great graven pine-cone of grey stone like the head of the Thyrsus of some colossal Dionysus turned to dust. Let it not be thought for a moment that I fail in loyalty to the butcher's shop, or that I am ashamed of the national sausage-machine. When I forget thee, O Drury Lane, may my right hand forget its cunning, or rather its clumsiness; for the fun of the English was clumsiness rather than cunning. Never shall I cease to boast of my hearty pleasure in all that heavy farce. I am merely drawing a distinction; and the Italian fantasy was different from the English farce; which the English have made English. The Continental comedy was not inappropriate to its own classical landscape. It was not incongruous even with the uniform of a guard outside the

Vatican Palace. Nor was the tradition of Pierrot anything like a heavy farce. It might rather be described as a light tragedy.

Now it is not fanciful to say that there is a real element of such dignity, and even of such tragedy, in the much greater gaiety of colour or bravado of outline in the serious symbols and decorations of the South; and especially in the military uniforms with their much franker parade of swinging sabre or tossing plume. We may sympathize with the British officers, who must escape from uniform; yet somehow do not escape from uniformity. But the South likes the uniform, not as a uniform, but as a contrast. It prefers the vanity, the valour and even the passions and pleasures of man to be picked out in flaming scarlet and yellow against the black background of death or destiny, and finds no relief in half-tones or twilight softness; any more than in wearing field-grey or brown to resemble the dust to which it shall return. It likes the figure that goes strutting with feather and sword, though it knows quite well that the sword may be as futile as the feather. That is why we of the north, when we first see such figures in such landscape, have the sense of something we can only call operatic. But we ought to remember that the name is associated with great things as well as small things; and certainly with serious things. Tragic and tremendous voices, shaking the heart and opening the depths of human nature like a day of judgment, have

come from what we call opera. And so they have from
this civilization of operatic colours and costumes. The
colours are bright because they are intense, not because
they are pale or diluted. We may compare it to an opera,
but not merely to a comic opera.

Therefore I do not apologize for the comparison that
came to my mind when I first saw the figure in stripes
standing at the top of the great grey stone staircase,
against the dark green gardens with their ornaments of
thyrsus and urn. If St. Francis of Assisi did not object to
being called the Juggler of God, I do not see why any
reasonable Swiss gentleman should object to being called
the Harlequin of the Pope. But as I watched him, and
the pale light from one of Rome's stormy days striking
his streaks of colour as he turned and shifted the hand
upon the halberd, something else stirred within me, to
which I could not as yet put a name. As these idle
thoughts had been drifting aimlessly through my mind,
there was an undercurrent in them that was somehow less
international and nearer home; something nameless connected with my own nation and even my own experience.
I could not imagine why this romantic Roman halberdier
should in any way remind me of England. I could recall
no connection except the unfortunate link of Sir Wil-
loughby Patterne; who was surely a blasting lightning
flash illuminating the Englishman abroad. He did not
approve of the Papal Guard. They were condemned by
his sense of humour, which he took very seriously. It cer-

tainly never occurred to him that the Papal Guard, lounging about and laughing in their motley uniforms, might themselves have been rather humorous about his sense of humour. But obviously that faint memory of Meredith was not the missing link in my mind; the link with London and my own early life. And then suddenly I remembered that long ago, in my older days of scribbling, I had written a ridiculous story about Notting Hill; of which the joke was that a man might die for a little suburb as if for a holy city; and that I had equipped the men fighting for it with the same sort of halberds and heraldic colours. The man standing on the great stairway was, among a myriad other more important things, one of my own little dreams come true. And I realized, with something rather like alarm at the coincidence, that the comparison might really have been pressed further. For the guard of the Vatican City really was defending a place almost parochial in size though the reverse of parochial in importance. That here in the heart of Christendom, on the high place of the whole world, on a plane above all earthly empires and under the white and awful light that strikes on an eternal town, was really a model state no larger than Notting Hill.

When it was first whispered that a compromise might restore the Temporal Power to the Pope, it is needless to say that a shock of apprehension went through the whole world, which had been discussing for fifty years what a dark and dreadful thing the Temporal Power had been. One could almost fancy that it was the only Temporal Power in the world; or at least (to be moderate) it was manifest to all that it must be in its nature more powerful than all the great Powers. The plans of the Pope for the conquest of the planet were not known in detail, except in some specially well informed wooden villages of the Middle West; but instant precautions were taken to prevent the celebrated Papal Galleys, rowed by thousands of slaves, from penetrating as far as Omaha or Kansas City. The situation was complicated through the discovery, by some who were electioneering against Al Smith, that he intended, if triumphant, to bring over the Pope to live as a permanent guest in the White House; which seems an indirect way of vigorously ruling Italy from the Vatican. But on the whole the followers of the more enlightened religions were fully warned of the danger. The Pope could not easily have bombarded New York or landed troops at Liverpool without somebody noticing it. Needless to say, most of his critics fell back on a general moral lamentation over the thought of any Christian pastor, though he were only a Roman Catholic, yielding to this imperial greed of conquest and laying down the cross to take up the sceptre and the sword. When they had said this at such length as seemed satisfactory and edifying, some of them began to ask what the Temporal Power was. Some of them, I was seriously told, actually asked for a map of Italy, showing the outlines of the Empire which the new Papal Emperor had seized; and they are puzzling over it still.

And indeed I do not blame them, for the Papal decision in the matter really is a puzzle in the sense of a paradox. Indeed it is so much of a paradox that the Papal action is by no means universally pleasing to Papists. Some certainly wish that the Temporal Power had been a little more powerful. I have been told that among the Romans especially there is something like a regret that they have not been more definitely distinguished from the rest of the world by some sort of link with the Roman Pontiff. Personally, I take the other view; but it is possible, to tell the truth, that I take it a little too personally. I think there is something both subtle and magnificent in the idea of claiming a foothold, but only a foothold, for the foot of St. Peter. A wild Futurist once wrote a romance called *The Aeroplane of The Pope;* and, speaking symbolically, there is really something wrong about the Pope being all up in the air, and dealing with all of the sky and none of the earth. But there is something strangely right about his claiming the smallest possible political power with the largest possible pontifical power. There is a sort of mathematical mystery about it; like the two extremes of the circumference and the central point. But I may be misled by my fancies, for I have always believed firmly in two things; the value of little states and local liberties, and the necessity of a general moral philosophy big enough to defend such little things. I cannot see how it is possible to hope for the liberty of little communities, unless there is a large theory of justice that is admitted by all communities. But I think it is singularly fitting that one of the very littlest should be the repository of the theory accepted by all the rest. I may be too romantic; and it is true, as I say, that I have sometimes in this matter dreamed dreams that were extravagant enough. But anyhow, there is something that I find enormously moving to my own imagination in the idea of that sacred island far inland, so small in its size, so absolute in its boundary, so strange and awful in its significance; the Holy Land of Europe; the minute microcosm of Christendom. And it mixes itself in some turbid fashion with all the old debates and dreams that I remember, touching liberty and limitations and the little commonwealths; as if the Faith were meant in this, as in so many things, to be at once a contradiction and an exaggeration and an example. It gives me a new thrill, when I accept the largest of all the religions, to salute it also as the smallest of the small nationalities.

That small piece of earth is indeed a sort of spiritual sublimate of the whole idea of justice that has made so many just men instinctively feel generous in the matter of small nationalities. It is the sense that it is the whole business of civilization to ensure the protection of small and precious things; that anarchism or taking anything, and imperialism or taking everything, are in their nature inferior to that finer sense of honour that deliberately re-

frains from taking something; that the tree of history is
judged by its fruits even when they look as small as
berries, and by its blossoms even when they look as
small as buds; that all humanity was subconsciously concerned to keep Athens and Florence and Jerusalem in-
tact; that the true spiral of imagination and creation is
always twisting inwards towards smaller and smaller
things, ever since men realized that jewels were smaller
than pebbles and seeds smaller than clods; that if there
be indeed a progress of humanity it may be such a
progress inwards to discover its own heart; that if there
be indeed an evolution, which means only an unfolding,
it may be like the unwrapping of some beautiful Christmas gift, in which large things only exist to be the box
and framework and protection of small; and that this
toy kingdom is indeed such a Christmas toy, since it is
not merely an exhibit in a museum but a relic in a shrine.

And when I realized that, I knew there had been something in my old nonsensical notion or novel, something
that was certainly never expressed properly in that novel
and almost certainly will never be expressed at all. I
can only hint at it by saying that what represents good
in this world must be first concrete and second compact.
The idealists and the professors of abstractions can never
understand it being concrete. The imperialists and the
greedy megalomaniacs can never understand it being
compact. The pearl of great price, in the parable, is as
valuable as a field or a kingdom, but it is not as vast as a

field or a kingdom. On the other hand, it is quite a mistake to suppose that because it is not more vast than the field, it is not more solid than the sky. The pearl is a possession, it is a positive and solid thing, it is an incomparably precious and priceless thing; only it is a small thing. But a thing; not a theory. And here indeed my thoughts began to drift towards deeper parallels where I dare hardly follow them, or at any rate follow them here; for the great supreme riddle or mystery which concentrates on that high place, or gathers against that citadel, in sunlight and lightning, all the blessings and curses of the world, is indeed the doctrine that what is most divine does truly offer itself as something as material and as small. Perhaps a truly great thing always tries to grow small; and there is hidden here a mystery of microscopic ambition. For though the Magnificat magnifies the Lord, it is only just after the Lord has minimized Himself. And there is here a mansion within a mansion, a new Bethlehem or House of Bread, and in the smallest of the tabernacles something yet more little than a child.

As I say, I find my words altogether fail me in following out the deepest applications of the principle; but I do believe there is some truth in that principle, concerning the material manifestation of good things; that it is material, but it is limited. When material things grow too large, men lose the sense that they are even material, and they take on the darker character of abstractions. Thus the measurement of the material universe, by modern science, by mere size, ceases to be real, and men do not believe that moons so far away are moons at all. So money may be merely mud, but mountains of money are something much worse than mud and far less than mountains. They become merely noughts in a ledger; that is the endless addition of nothing to nothing. The vulgar American expression about delivering the goods has this dim truth about it; that good does express itself in goods, but not in too many goods. States that are small enough to be really governed, properties that are small enough to be really owned, works of art that are concrete and compact enough to be permanently appreciated, these are a class of things which the vast capitalist organizations of to-day understand very little, but which Italy of the small republics and the little vineyards has understood very well. And as my wandering thoughts went back to the solitary figure on the steps, which had so inconsequently called them forth, I remembered that he was also the representative of many brave men who have really defended such tiny towns with such old-world weapons. For though in one sense his sword and halberd are harmless and for show, yet he or his like have died on those steps in defence of the Father of Christians; and if need were, which God avert, the Harlequin would die again.

But he will hardly have to die. Many are asking, in effect, what the new Vatican State or Roman Settlement means. I can tell them at least one thing that it means.

It means that nobody is going to make the mistake again which the whole nineteenth century made. Even the survivors who made the mistake will now probably deny that they ever made it. For this is a very practical side of history that is generally entirely forgotten; in this case, as I say, wilfully forgotten. Real history, if there could be such a thing, would not consist of what men did or even what they said. It would consist far more of the mighty and enormous things that they did not say. The assumptions of an age are more vital than the acts of an age. The most important sentence is the sentence that a whole generation has forgotten to say; or felt it needless to say. It is that silence which so often makes a whole generation inscrutable, and leaves the sons looking in the faces of strange fathers. The men from the middle of the eighteenth century to the middle of the nineteenth had a luminous but negative notion, which most of them expressed with polite moderation; but which they expressed better, perhaps, in water colour sketches of broken aqueducts in the Campagna or carefully shaded drawings of sculptured fragments in the Vatican. Rogers the wit, who in some strange way came to be called a poet, doing all the elegant things required of him by his world, wrote verses about Italian landscape and history; verses as smooth-sliding as Mincius but hardly crowned with the vocal reeds of Milton. It is significant of the spirit in which these men wrote of such things that he called his poem "The Pleasures of Memory." That generation wrote of other things under the title of "The Pleasures of Hope." Rome to these men in most aspects, but supremely in its religious aspect, was at best a memory; still a respected memory, but always a fading memory. But Rogers the wit, as distinct from Rogers the poet, was also the man who made the famous remark that he believed in the religion of all sensible men; and when asked what it was, replied placidly: "Sensible men never say."

There he bore witness to one of these universal silences of which I speak. Rogers himself meant, quite simply, that his religion was irreligion. But all the men of that time meant that it was something less like the old Roman religion than they commonly said in so many words. All the sensible men assumed that the world would abandon such beliefs if it became more sensible; and most of them assumed that it would become more sensible. That is the point to see about this substantial if subconscious agreement. Nearly all of them thought that such religion, which they would call superstition, was not only a dream but a dream from which everybody was waking up. Most of them were polite to it; some of them were rude to it; but hardly any of them really expected it to last another hundred years. The vast majority of them thought that it would die; without saying so. Now they know that it will live; also without saying so.

Every great man of the nineteenth century made that mistake, and only a few unmade it. Every great dictator from Napoleon to Bismarck, blundered sooner or later on that particular point. Napoleon, being a man of far finer culture and intelligence than Bismarck, found himself in the midst of the misunderstanding; and before the end understood that he had misunderstood. Bismarck, I suppose, never understood the name of the rock that had tripped and thrown him. But both of them, and all of them, fell down on this fact; that they fancied that in some way the Papacy was connected with the Past. The Papacy is as much a thing of the Future as a thing of the Past; it is very sharply and plainly a thing of the Present. It may be a menace of the Future; it may be a plague of the Present; so far as that argument is concerned, it may be a new peril like the Next War or the Final Comet. It may be Antichrist coming in the last days and bestriding the earth with a new and evil empire, as is sometimes whispered with confidential excitement by men who hand round little leaflets at Margate. But it is not a ruin or a broken arch in the middle of the Campagna, to be sketched in water colours or lamented in elegiacs. Everybody knows that now, whether they say so or not; and the men nearest to it know it best of all. And *that,* for one thing, is the meaning of the Vatican State.

Compare the conduct of dictators like Napoleon and Bismarck with the conduct of dictators like Mussolini and Pilsudski. The former thought that they were falling over so much lumber and that the lumber would soon be cleared away. The latter know that they are coming against certain limits; and those limits will never be moved away. They may like or dislike them in varying degrees; they may bargain with them or balance them with various alternatives, but they will always deal with the Papacy as they would deal with the Pyrenees or the Polar Sea; in short, as they deal with the planet and everything that will only end with the planet. That is the lesson that has been learnt by the strong men of the age once dedicated to the production of the Superman. That is the chief difference between the nineteenth century and the twentieth. That is the news silently digested by those whose information and outlook are really new. Here is the wisdom of the new dictators; that they do know where they cannot dictate.

For the moment, the signal of that discovery is a tiny scrap of territory not much larger than its own flag; but its flag is its own. Its purpose and policy are its own; it is visible, it is inviolable, it is saluted by all the flags of the world. And it represents primarily this profound change in the historic sense of Europeans. That notion that old things can always be left behind has itself been left behind. The notion that what is traditional is destructible is itself destroyed; the notion that all our Christian past was dying is dead.

In short, Mussolini may not be a greater man than Napoleon, but he is a wiser man than Napoleon; a hundred years wiser. And the difference is exactly this; that a hundred years ago all men held their breath and said: "The Pope has crossed the path of Napoleon." But if there were an internal quarrel in Italy to-morrow (*absit omen*) the same men would hold their breath and say: "Mussolini has crossed the path of the Pope." The notion of something permanent in European affairs, not to be altered even by right and just revolutions, has come with a quiet and crushing force to all our contemporaries, and especially to the most intelligent and even the most revolutionary. Henceforth, the more a man wants to destroy something that ought to be destroyed, the less he will turn aside to be entangled in an attempt to destroy the indestructible. Napoleon could have brought back common sense and the career open to talent, sweeping away the stiff and frozen frivolities of a feudalism already dead for ages, without going out of his way to pretend that the Pope was not the Pope. But he was a man of his time and could not always resist the contemporary illusion that the Papacy was the Past. *Qui mange du Pape meurt;* but this great man discovered his error before dying, and certainly adjured it in the hour of death. Bismarck might have announced that a German Empire was born without wantonly adding that the Papal Empire was dying; but he also was a simple man of his time, and was patiently watching for it to die. The new men of action have grown tired of watching and waiting to see the death of undying things; and, while quite capable of dealing death, will leave alone the specialist function of dealing damnation round the land. In a sense it means the first appearance of secular government in the modern

[271]

world or, in other words, of government that minds its own business.

An anti-clerical government is not a secular government. It is the very reverse of secular or even secularist. Anti-clericalism is a particular form of religious bigotry intruding and intriguing in secular politics. It is opposed to Catholicism as was Calvinism; but with exactly the same poison of spirituality in the wrong place. Anti-clericalism keeps countries like France in a perpetual ferment of debate about God and the things that are God's; and tends if anything to prevent people from rendering to Cæsar the things that are Cæsar's. There is nobody so theistic as the atheist; just as in the last resort there is nobody so mystical as the materialist. The French atheist has wasted so much time talking of what he says does not exist, that he has no right to be annoyed when an Italian Syndicalist suddenly jumps up and proposes to discuss things that do exist. But there is one thing which the Italian Syndicalist very early recognized as being among the things that do exist; and, even while not yet especially his affair, as a thing that would go on existing. It is real realism; it is the spread of the scientific spirit in politics; which has revealed in the geological formation of southern Europe something which men in a less scientific age thought to trample like mire or drive before them like dust; a rock.

Modern Italy is a model of how the state becomes so much more secular by becoming less secularist. Even

Rome, in which there seem sometimes to be more churches than houses, almost takes on the appearance of a sensible secular town. It could not do so while the very name of Nathan recalled the Jewish Prophet—and the Jewish Problem. It could not do so while that remarkable Jewish Prophet stood in permanent antithesis to the Christian Apostle. Rome has become a rational place where policemen are policemen and priests are priests and soldiers are soldiers; not a place where they are clericals or anti-clericals. Some of them may be atheists but not many of them are lunatics; like the lunatics who made black marks against the name of any French soldier who went to church, and who nearly lost the Great War in order to spite the spiritual tastes of Foch. This sort of rationality is not necessarily religion, certainly not my religion; and it may have a long way to go before it becomes internally religious. But it is something to have seen the dawn of a new Age of Reason, and a real race of rationalists who will leave religion alone.

It is the whole point of this book that the pomps of Rome are rightly meaningless until we know what they mean. I am entirely on the side of the Puritan who thinks the symbol fictitious so long as he thinks the significance false. I am now going to attempt to describe the personal experience of approaching the very centre of such pomps or ceremonies, and meeting the personal ruler who oversees them all. I am particularly anxious to affirm, at the start, that though of course these shows and pageants meant immeasurably much to me, and profoundly affected my emotions, yet I do not base my belief on such emotions, still less on such pageants or shows. I was myself received into the Catholic Church in a small tin shed, painted brick-red, which stood among the sculleries and outhouses of a Railway Hotel. That represents with great exactitude the precise extent to which I was or am influenced by exquisite architecture or alluring music or storied windows richly dight, casting a dim religious light. And the Pope would be the first to say that the step I took in entering that shed was inconceivably more important than the step of entering St. Peter's, or the Vatican, or his own presence.

I saw His Holiness Pius XI three times; the first time in private audience; the second in a semi-private assembly of various notables; and the third time among the crowds that thronged St. Peter's on the day of the Beatification of the English Martyrs. On the first occasion a dignitary who was the head of one of the National Colleges kindly helped to introduce me; and I have seldom been more grateful for human companionship. It is altogether inadequate to say I was nervous. I was nervous when I saw Signor Mussolini, chiefly because he talked French so much better than I did. But it is perhaps curious to note that, while my nervousness in the presence of Il Duce drove me madly on to talk French and more French, merely because I could not talk French, I found in the presence of the Pope that I could not talk English, or talk at all. He came suddenly out of his study, a sturdy figure in a cape, with a square face and spectacles, and began speaking to me about what I had written, saying some very generous things about a sketch I wrote of St. Francis of Assisi. He asked me if I wrote a great deal; and I answered in fragmentary French phrases that it was only too true, or words to that effect. The clerical dignitary nobly struck in in my support by saying it was my modesty. As a matter of fact, my head was in a whirl and it might have been anything. Then he made a motion and we all knelt; and in the words that followed I understood for the first time something that was once meant by the ceremonial use of the plural; and in a flash I saw the sense of something that had always seemed to me a senseless custom of kings. With a new strong voice, that was hardly even like his own, he began "Nous vous benissons," and I knew that something stood there infinitely greater than an individual; I knew that it was indeed "We"; We, Peter and Gregory and Hildebrand and all the dynasty that does not die. Then, as he passed on, we rose and found our way out of the Palace, through knots of Swiss and Papal Guards, till we were again under the open sky. I said to the clerical dignitary, "That frightened me more than anything I have known in my life." The clerical dignitary laughed heartily.

One touch may be added to the scene, which is not so irrelevant as it looks. When we left the Vatican, one of

the party discovered the loss of an umbrella; I
somebody else's umbrella. With all respect
umbrella, I thought it unlikely that it would be
a Papal canopy and carried in state in any of th
geous processions. But we made the obvious jest
the highest church dignitaries having a weakne
stealing umbrellas, or having a little horde of pa
Then some one more native to the spot said firml
the Pope would certainly give it to the niggers. "
moment," said my informant solemnly, "a little
is walking about in the sun with your umbrell
this slightly exaggerative form I first fully realize
quality to be added to the obvious qualities of Pi
it is called an enthusiasm for missions, but it is i
a very strong antagonism to the contempt for the a
inal races and a gigantic faith in the fraternity of all
in the light of the Faith. "We have not only to save
tendom, but to save mankind." A distinguished S
navian, whom I met later, was so warm an uphol
this humanitarianism that he said, with shining e
one who beholds a vision, "We may yet have a
Pope." In a spirit of disgraceful compromise, I sugg
meekly that (if not quite ready for that) I should l
lighted to see a black Cardinal. I was conscious of
shadowy pleasure in the image; and I recalle
imperial bust of black marble with the red robe
wondered if there is something prophetic or signi
in our fancies. Then I remembered the great King

to Bethlehem, heavy with purple and crimson and
a face like night; and I was ashamed.

second time I saw the Pope with more detachment,
eard him at greater length; when the documents of
eatification were finally read for his approval. I
the very long list of those English heroes, who re-
the despotic destruction of the national religion,
a due order; and listened to a number of names that
ed like Smith or Higgins pronounced with a per-
talian accent. Then the Pope himself spoke, in a
er rather conversational than rhetorical, but with
little Italian gesture and vivacity, by the standard
glish conversation. What moved me very much, as
aglishman and an exile, was that he spoke with
ar warmth and vividness in praise of England, and
ne who had seen it rather than heard of it. He
even more strongly on the words, "So beautiful a
ry," than on the words, "So great a nation." He also
asized strongly the fact that the last witnesses in
nd were men of every class and condition, poor as
s rich, and agricultural labourers as well as the first
of the land. He spoke in Italian; but so clearly and
such exact gesture that I could understand nearly
word.

ly, as I have said, the last time I saw him was in
llest blaze of publicity when he came to consum-
the Beatification before a colossal congregation, and
aclude it by celebrating Benediction at the High

Altar. Here indeed there was, admittedly and openly, the full torrent of pomp and popular excitement; but it seemed to me as if I already knew enough not to trust merely to the effect of these. Pius XI will always be to me a real man whom I have met; with all the intense but indescribable difference that that fact makes in our judgment of men. I should always know that certain things said about him were nonsense; it is true, in that sense, that pageantry proves nothing one way or the other; and he might be enthroned on the top of St. Peter's, with populations lying prostrate round it for miles, and I should still know that there was not in him any shadow of pride. Nevertheless, the pageant as a pageant is well worthy of better words than I can find for it, for it had another significance also, which perhaps can only be suggested in another way. It begins so far away that I can only convey it by getting far away from it.

The historic Church, which contains all things, contains something not only historic, but prehistoric. It is awful with the Primitive Revelation, and even the Fall or the Flood. I came to feel it in the most barbaric of the Baroque; and in the Baldacchino in St. Peter's, which I once hated, is a piece of black confectionery of twisted sticks of liquorice. But when, as I shall describe, a voice like a great wind went through the central temple of the world, I suddenly felt that its dark spirals were dizzy like tropic trees, in some boiling cyclone of the south; when something beyond words shakes the dark heart of

Africa; something that is Worship—yes, if it be only devil-worship.

When I made a due and proper pilgrimage to the Lake of Nemi, it was chiefly for the sake of something that is not there. It was combined, I grieve to say, with a certain momentary indifference verging on irritation, concerning what is there. I have explained with all humility that I am a bad sight-seer, without intending any reflection on the sight-seers or the sights. The power of abruptly adapting the proper sentiment to the present sight may be a form of presence of mind which it is a weakness to lack; but anyhow I lack it. Therefore I went to Nemi with the secret gratification of knowing that my own favourite sight is not there to be seen. Most sensible people go there to see what is to be seen of the Galleys of Caligula, but somehow I felt curiously cold about these vessels, as if they were the house-boats of Sir Thomas Lipton. Caligula seems modern in so many ways; he was mad and doubtless spent a great deal of money on show, in things like these particular ships. But the name of Nemi was connected in my mind with that dark primeval cult of the priest of the moon; who was ordained for his sacred office by becoming a murderer and then looking forward as cheerfully as possible to being murdered. I looked at Nemi as the scene of that mystery, and even in bright sunshine it was worthy of it. It really is "the still glassy lake that sleeps beneath Aricia's trees," though Macaulay did say so. But the absence of the temple, so

much more impressive than the presence of the galle
minded me of something else which is not irreleva
this rambling theme.

Amid the million sensational novels which I hav
voured with the most agreeable sensations, I reme
one which was really very thrilling; and the thrill
sisted in the well concealed and well betrayed secret
there still exists in the world a group continuin
ancient and mysterious rite of Nemi; the temple of I
where the priest sacrificed the priest. The story w
well told that the reader did really feel something
the icy shock of antiquity. He realized something
naturally moving in the mere fact that a religion
somehow managed to survive out of ancient R
times. Few of those who read that novel would
to reflect that a religion really has survived out of ar
Roman times. But nobody notices it, because it i
secret but public; because it is not cruel but humane
because in that antique Italian idolatry, it is not the
but the god that died.

Nevertheless, it is only by some such angle almo
accident, that it is possible to put a finger on that
of fear and unfamiliarity, by which we can really a
the stupendous fact that has happened. In one sens
idiots are perfectly right when they say that the C
tian religion is but a continuation of the Pagan relig
Only it was nothing in the Pagan religions them
that could possibly continue. It was in itself a Chr

to make Paganism live. When we look at the
we see something that the heathens saw; the only
that remains of them or their seeing. Despite the
s of the detective narrative I have mentioned, we
f us know very well that there is not a modern
f Diana quietly cutting the throat of the late in-
t of his parish. But there is something pretty
as old and every bit as sensational. The story is
ly a romance, it is in the first derivative sense a
in that it is still novel, or has not left off being

first example of this is that the very garments of
ests standing at the altar are essentially the gar-
of a man of ancient Rome, or even of heathen
In being handed down for hundreds and hun-
of years, they have of course been modified in
, but they preserve the ancient plan. What looks
nge to us in a man standing at the altar would
have looked so strange to Horace or Catullus in
walking in the street. The whole apparatus of
nd priest and sacred enclosure carries us back to
hich seems to us like the world before the Flood,
remoteness we really express when we can only
Antiquity. On the day of the Beatification, as this
vious idea crossed my mind when gazing at those
o serve in the sanctuary, I looked round at the
ariegated and many-coloured crowd in the church,
ll their multifarious uniforms and robes of office.

And it struck me as odd, even at a glance, to note that there were people present in almost every costume of every century since that first garb of Antiquity had been worn. We all know how a past period will leave behind one feature like a fossil; how Beef-Eaters wear the uniform of guards under Henry VIII or Bluecoat Boys wear the garments of boys under Edward VI. But here it was not a question of one or two survivals in incongruous clothes. All the generations of men were here, and most of them still playing a part congruous to their original purpose. The Franciscans, in their brown and corded frocks, were simply peasants of the early Middle Ages; unaltered since St. Francis changed clothes with a peasant. The men who immediately surround the Pope, and carry his throne, seemed quite familiar figures in square-cut garments of Genoese velvet; for we have seen them in hundreds of pictures. They were simply men of the Renaissance, whose dark red garments have glowed in countless canvases of Titian or Veronese. In a ring outside these stood men so startlingly like academy pictures of Essex and Raleigh that for a moment one might suppose it was a highly historical carnival; yet these were not fancy dresses but the ancient ceremonial dress of old orders of knighthood or offices of piety handed down for three hundred years. They stood in their stiff ruffs and ribbed trunk hose with all that easy gravity of men wearing their own proper clothes, as if they were standing about in the court of Philip II of Spain. So it was right down the ages; there were later types with the knee-breeches and court swords of the eighteenth century, and others in an evening dress to us rather reminiscent of the nineteenth century; and behind, the huge twentieth century crowd, with the clothes of our own day. Pageantry, as I say, is little enough in itself; but if you are talking of pageantry, there never was a pageant in the world like this; for it is a procession of all the centuries, not of actors dressed up as dead things, but of things really dating from those centuries and yet alive. As the vast throng moved by, I caught a glimpse beyond of the coloured image of Our Lady, and the words went through my mind: "All generations shall call me blessed."

The greater part of this solemn carnival of all the sons of time moved forward vaguely like a vast wave, far ahead of the actual termination of the triumph, which was the appearance of the Pontiff. And as I looked and listened, I realized a paradox that inheres in the very nature of that place. St. Peter's looks fairly large, but it is very much larger than it looks. Some have praised it for this, as being a triumph of proportion; some have scoffed at it for this, like Macaulay when he said that an architect so clever as to make a big building look small is as sensible as a debater so clever as to make a strong argument look weak. But whatever be our view of the fact, it certainly is the fact. Something in the curious cavernous lines of the place, with its wide and curved and almost wavering pillars, make us imagine something lowering

[283]

over our heads or enclosing us in dizzy and magic circles which is not the same as the mere sensation of unlimited space. There is a sort of optical illusion, which is here corrected by what I may call an auricular confession. Suddenly, I realized that my ears contradicted my eyes. For there came as if carried on the wind something that was almost a whisper; and yet I knew by the thrill of it that it was a shout. It was the people at the other end of the church cheering the Pope; but it was like the sound of people cheering whole streets away. There was something creepy at once in the contradiction and the realization. It was as if a man called across the room and his voice seemed to come faint and far across the valley. And with the sound of that the whole building seemed to swell and expand and open upwards into eternity, until we realized that these painted and gilded caverns were vast like the hollows of the sky. The noise grew louder and louder along a remote and winding road; and at last, while it was yet distant, rose into one deafening roar of "Viva Il Papa." Perhaps it was an accident; but I did not hear anywhere that cry that used to be provocative and political in the days of the division: "Viva Il Papa-Re." Perhaps it was felt to be in bad taste to insist on it, now that the nation and the Holy Father were friends. Perhaps it was because there was no need for it now. He was a King and need not be called so. Anyhow the roar rose as if to rend the roof as the Pope passed by. Officially, I believe, the congregation were forbidden to shout. God knows what noise they would have made, if they had been allowed to shout.

Of that which thus passed, and was thus saluted, there is another word to be said, or the full impression will be again false. I have already referred to the real case for popular pomp in an institution like the Papacy; and have admitted as a fact, and defended as a logical fact, that it does hold itself free to go almost all lengths in material magnificence. And yet, if we left the matter thus, we should miss yet a further point. There is in fact a further paradox; very illustrative of the immemorial instincts of hieratic art. It must be remembered that, even among heathens, it is perhaps the oldest art in the world. The instincts and imagination behind it are very deep and delicate; and there is a sense in which the Pontifex Maximus is the simplest figure in the scene. There is something analogous to things lifted into a clearer and a colder air, in the tradition by which a pale and silver splendour has been made the high light of the picture. It passes into a phase where light has transcended colour; as in the hueless dawn of creation when the first light was as strange as the first snow, or like the last white ashes of a world purified by death. There is here something subtle, altogether above the scale of pride and isolated by its very background of glory; where he walks in white when all his household is clothed in scarlet; and moves to the sound of trumpets; but they are of silver and not of brass or gold.

Whatever that pageant may mean, it has passed like a vision, and if there were no more to say of its meaning, we could agree that it is passed like a dream. Nobody but a fool, I respectfully repeat, would take such shows and shadows as a reason for his belief; but when belief has once satisfied the reason, it would be strange indeed if these things did not follow and pursue with all the wings of the imagination. Nor does the outer world disdain to be inspired by ceremony; it only invents other ceremonies that are not so inspiring. We talk of anti-ritualists, but there are no anti-ritualists. It is only given to men to degrade ritualism into etiquette. And when we went forth from that place into the world outside, with its advertisements and its newspapers and its flunkeys and its fashionable dresses, we cannot be very much blamed if we thought that the world within had held something larger than the world without.

Yet, strangely enough, it is exactly at this moment that I can turn once more and say a word of consolation to my invisible companion, my dear friend the Nordic Man, the cultivated tourist, whether he be Puritan or Ruskinian or grim unsoftened Gothicist, with whom (you must know) I have been wandering hand in hand from the beginning of this book and through all the streets of this city. To him alone I have been appealing and attempting to demonstrate (quite without effect) that the tone of triumph and parade which he feels in the monuments of the Papal city is not quite so worthless, or at least not quite so meaningless as he thinks. For his ear alone have been the digressions and examples, in which I sought to suggest that all this triumph is not mere vainglory, because the fight and the triumph were not vain. I have hinted to him that a city and a civilization does really rejoice over certain great Pontifical judgments; from the Pope in the ninth century who justified Statues to the Pope in the nineteenth century who justified Strikes. And all the time I was thus reasoning with him, in so affectionate a fashion, I fear that his Nordic spirits have sunk lower and lower; and that he has found it hardest of all to pardon my recent laudation of the coloured pageant in St. Peter's. Well, I will end by making an admission, I might almost say by telling a secret; though I know not whether that, when explained, will make it easier for us to part friends. Much as I felt the majesty of the Papal procession, keenly as I shared the enthusiasm for the cause of the English Martyrs, these were not the scenes that have remained most magnetically in my memory, nor the inward pictures which I shall recall till I die. As I said at the beginning, the objects that really please the traveller are often apparently detached and illogical; there is no man so self-controlled as to be sure of feeling his most intense emotions at the most important time. I will conclude by confessing that two other images, the one transitory, the other familiar, now stand out from all my impressions with the prominence of something mesmeric and with a power akin to magic. I will leave them with the reader, hoping that here, after all, the lost meaning may be found.

Some time before we left Rome, the city was illuminated everywhere for the festival of the Immaculate Conception. The doctrine is not in question here, but it is worth noting, in relation to the general theme, that it is a recent and almost defiant decision, right or wrong, made in the very midst of the rationalist or anti-clerical nineteenth century, as a challenge to the world from a religion that refused to die. In any case, to see a celebration of this sort in the heart of Southern civilization is to have nothing left but laughter for those who pretend that Catholicism is Puritan and not popular or festive. There was, of course, every kind of decoration and display, down to those which have for us almost grotesque associations. There were fireworks; and I have always been as fond of fireworks as a child or a Chinaman. Nor could I, at any time of my life, have found it easy to maintain that the love of Mary was a less worthy motive than the hatred of Guy Fawkes. But I do not speak of the general brilliance that burned through the heart of the night, but of one chance effect, which (as I have said) fixed itself in my memory with an intensity quite indescribable. Which is the reason (of course) that I shall here show the weakness of all writing men, by attempting to describe it.

I had always had, I hardly know why, a sort of attachment to that particular column near the Piazza di Spagna, which is topped by a figure of the Virgin standing on the crescent of the moon. When I came on it, on this particular night, as it rose into the dark dome of sky above the pale or painted façades of the Italian houses, it was picked out more distinctly by one of the long searchlights, but still so delicately that the grey stone was barely changed to a faint silver; it might have been moonshine and fitting enough to the statue thus standing on the moon. But when I looked up at the moon, I could not see it. For it seemed at first to be caught or entangled in incredible many-coloured clouds; such coloured clouds as are never seen against the vault of night. When I looked again, I felt as if it were a miracle; and a more amazing miracle than sunset clouds at midnight. For these things were not many-coloured clouds but banks of many-coloured blossom. It seemed as if Our Lady had at that instant alighted, and the stark stone pillar had broken into flowers under her feet. (No, no, dear Nordic companion, I did not *think* it was a miracle. There is no need for us to discuss the dead philosophy of monism and materialism.) What did I think it was? What shall I say, or what shall anybody say?

> What are the names for Beauty? Who shall praise
> God's pledge He can fulfil His creature's eyes?
> Or what strong words of what creative phrase
> Determine Beauty's title in the skies?

The question put in Mr. Belloc's sonnet is the only

answer to any other question in this case. We have all seen flowers. We have all seen statues and columns. We have all seen moonlight. These things, or words, do not convey in separation even the most remote suggestion of that amazing garden in the sky. The wan light lay on it like a veil, not discolouring and yet changing as by enchantment; so that while nothing was lost of the glow from the glorious flowers of Italy, they had also something unearthly and luminous that might belong to the flowers of the moon. The little meadow on which She walked seemed infinitely far away in the upper void of space; and yet the Figure seemed to have come nearer.

Was I worshipping the image? No. Oh, no. Only with *dulia*. Not with *latria*. Did I know that the column and also the statue were only two large pieces of stone? I did. Was I aware that modern science, in her ruthless researches into the laws of nature, has discovered that flowers do not generally grow out of bare stone, when there is no earth for them to grow out of? I was. Has this anything to do with any intelligent person offering his homage to such a vision, as to something sent by God? It has not. I am quite well acquainted, thank you, with the fact that Protestantism denounces idolatry. I am also acquainted with the fact that Catholicism forbids idolatry. But wherever and in whatever mode or form my prayers were offered, they included a prayer that somehow or somewhere there might be found enough daylight or dynamite to lift the prigs and provincials who ask such questions a hundred leagues into the upper air; far and wide into those wider and more windy altitudes where She stands, beholding, before we can see it, the broad dawn that is breaking over Christendom; that the poor fellows may, for once, be really In Advance of the Age; and travelling through time as well as space, find the paradise where, far above the roofs of Rome in winter, She walked upon the flowers of spring.

Whether you call it accident or art or artifice, there was something much more than conventional ornament in the idea of heaping those burning blossoms on the precipice of that remote pillar. I mention the detail without any inferences; but when I asked who had done it, I was told that the flowers before this image were the personal contribution of Mussolini.

I have not written this book for those who like Rome; those who like Rome know infinitely more about it than I do; and even I have not dealt here with the details of what I know. I have not written it for those who pretend to like Rome, for they will not admit the difficulty with which I deal; and there is no fate or fashion compelling them to pretend to like my books. I have certainly not written it for those mysterious people who definitely dislike Rome, and yet think it their duty to come from the ends of the earth and examine everything in it. I have written it for those who would like to like Rome, but feel an honest temptation to dislike it, for the perfectly just and adequate reason that they cannot make out what it is all about. And my own difficulty is that, though I believe my own thesis of perpetual Resurrection is the real clue, I cannot easily point to any lucid and conscious expression of that thesis; the jungle is too thick and gorgeous for the primitive roots to be seen. Rome has hidden herself in her hundred innovations and renewals, and has given many a man the impression rather of walking amid the ruins of old revolutions than in the scheme or scaffolding of new plans for the world. As a fact, the new plans in Rome are as plain as the old ones; but they also are put forth by men too eager to explain themselves, and likely to leave behind them great works, which may in their turn be great ruins, but will almost certainly be great riddles. It is not easy to find the place where Rome has hidden the key to the riddle; in the form of any simple summary of the central idea. Critics of the New Italy, or the new social experiments, may be as crude as those who imagine that, because silver trumpets are blown before the Pope, therefore he is always blowing his own trumpet.

And at last, I might almost say by accident, in the course of my very irregular and indeed insufficient wanderings among the classical fanes of the most famous of earthly cities, I came upon the exact expression of all that I have here been vainly trying to express. I have done my best to explain that I do not blame the traveller who can see nothing but what is blatant and empty in all those hollow horns and urns and tossing trumpets, which seem to him hollow in the same fashion as the florid masks of tragedy and comedy. I have also done my best to explain that these things are anything but hollow, save with the hollowness of drums and bugles going into battle. I have tried to sketch here and there the nature of the battle and the reason of the triumph. But here, in this one place, is an older type of symbolism, in which the real nature of that triumph is conveyed as I can hardly convey it here. It is traced in mosaic in the apse of the ancient church of St. Clemente, one of the most remarkable and yet one of the most typically Roman of churches; for it descends below into a stratification of dead churches and pagan foundations. Under all there is a dark cavern carved with the mystery of Mithras; and I have heard, standing before that strange altar, the noise of the Lost Waters of Rome. But the upper church, in which I have heard Mass, is in more ways than one the crown of the revival and triumph of Christian things; and the old decoration of the apse expresses the idea with a symmetry that is almost startling. The apse is a half-moon of gold on the usual pattern; but at the top there is a cloud out of which comes the hand of God above the crucifix. It does not merely bless it or even merely rest on it. It seems to take the cross as if by the cross-hilt and thrust it like a sword into the earth below. Yet in one sense it is the very reverse of a sword, since its touch is not death but life; life springing and sprouting and shooting into the air, that the world may have life, and that it may have it more abundantly.

It is impossible to say too much of the fruitful violence of this effect. It is not the normal groping of roots or branches. It is more like the blood of the earth spurting instantly from its arteries at the first wound. The living shoots go whirling away into space covering the whole background with their gyres and eddies; as if to lassoo the stars. This antique design does really achieve what so many Futurist experiments or crazy jazz decorations have attempted; to make a dynamic diagram and to express suddenness in a pattern. The very disproportion between the long loops and circles sprawling everywhere and the slender cross at whose touch they have leapt into life, emphasizes with energy the power of that magic wand. Curled inside each of the circles, as in something that is at once a nest and a new and separate world, is a bird, to express the universal birth of life; and each bird is different in species or colour. No one but a madman could stand before it and say that our faith is anti-vital or a creed of death. And there is one last touch, which has already been remarked by many; that the face of the Crucified, which in most images is naturally tragic, is in this case radiant and like the sun at noon; or like the words that have no need to be written here in any motto or inscription: I am the Resurrection and the Life.

THE END